Florida Golf Getaways

Saddlebrook Resort

Florida Golf Getaways

By Edward Schmidt, Jr.

SENTINEL BOOKS

A publication of The Orlando Sentinel
Sentinel Books
Orlando/1990

Copyright © 1990
Sentinel Communications Company
633 N. Orange Avenue, Orlando, Florida 32801

Edited by Ken Paskman
Designed by Eileen Schechner

Cover photograph of Orlando Marriott World Center by Red Huber
Back cover photograph by Red Huber
Photographs courtesy of resorts and advertising agencies
Illustrations by Gerald Masters

Printed in the United States

First edition 1990

Library of Congress Cataloguing-in-Publication No. 90-61564

ISBN 0-941263-12-6

About The Author

Edward Schmidt, Jr., a golf and travel writer based in Orlando, Fla., has written more than 200 articles for regional, national and international publications. He is a member of the Golf Writers Association of America and is real estate editor for *Golfweek* newspaper. His articles have appeared in *Golf Illustrated, Florida Golfer, Successful Meetings* and many other publications.

Dedication

To my wife, Diane, Mom, Dad and
my brother Paul, who taught me
the wonders of golf and life.

Acknowledgments

Special thanks to the Florida
Division of Tourism, George
Biggers III, Ken Paskman, Eileen
Schechner, Bethany Mott, Bill
Altice, Bryan Heliker, Sol Bayouth
and Dave Murray.

Thanks also to Orlando Marriott
World Center, Grand Cypress
Resort, Universal Air Service and
The Orlando Sentinel Camera
Department.

Contents

Introduction
Page 13

About this guide
Page 15

Chapter 1: Planning a Florida golf getaway
Page 16

Chapter 2: The resort course
Page 20

Chapter 3: Northwest Florida
Page 26

Chapter 4: Northeast Florida
Page 39

Chapter 5: Central Florida
Page 56

Chapter 6: Upper West Coast Florida
Page 77

Chapter 7: Southwest Florida
Page 90

Chapter 8: Southeast Florida
Page 107

Chapter 9: The Florida golf lifestyle
Page 135

Chapter 10: Your Florida golf source
Page 140

Index
Page 143

Introduction

Perdido Bay

The combination of pleasant weather, a tropical lifestyle and superb golf courses has attracted more than a few golfers to Florida. To be sure, pros like Jack Nicklaus (North Palm Beach), Arnold Palmer (Orlando), Gary Player (Orlando) and Raymond Floyd (Miami) don't live in the Sunshine State just so they can have a year-round tan.

No, it's quality golf that appeals to these giants of the game, as well as other professional golfers. At last count, 64 of the regular PGA Tour players called Florida home, and the state is the most popular residential location for PGA Senior Tour players. In addition, several of the world's most distinguished golf course architects reside in Florida, including Bill Amick, Lloyd Clifton, Pete Dye, Ron Garl, Tom Fazio, Mark McCumber, Joe Lee and Ed Seay.

Golf is the lure for many other residents and visitors, too. According to the National Golf Foundation's 1989 figures, more than 1 million Florida residents play golf. Also, more than 1.8 million visitors played golf in Florida in '89. In fact, Florida led the way as the most frequented golf destination in 1989. It was twice as popular as its nearest rivals, Arizona and South Carolina, and three times as popular as California and North Carolina.

The Sunshine State has more golf courses than any other state. Of the nation's more than 13,500 courses, Florida has 1,000, with many more on the way.

For the visitor who wants to experience the wonders of Florida golf, the state's magnificent, amenity-rich, golf-oriented resorts and semiprivate residential courses offer the game at an unparalleled level. Nowhere else in the world is golf such an integral part of the tourism infrastructure of a region as it is in Florida.

Diversity is the key when talking about Florida courses. In the northern region there are rolling hills and pines; in the south it's flat and sandy. Oceanside, hilly and lakeside layouts are scattered throughout the state. No matter what your design preference — traditional, modern or Scottish — you'll find it in Florida.

Finally, I'd like to address my golf game. I'm a golf junkie. Unfortunately, that doesn't mean I'm a great golfer. Far from it. I'm a golf writer, with heavy emphasis on the latter. Reportedly, the national average score for 18 holes is 91, and I generally shoot a couple of strokes on either side of that number.

This book is a culmination of several years of "research." I've struggled for 5 hours on Pete Dye's unforgiving TPC Stadium Course at Sawgrass, hit the long ball on the never-ending fairways at Grenelefe's West course, and landed in so many pot bunkers at Grand Cypress Resort's New Course I thought I was on a combat mission. Despite my occasional futility, I had a marvelous time playing these and other remarkable Florida courses.

Regardless of your skill level, I think you'll enjoy yourself, too. And even if you have one of those days when you run out of balls by the 15th hole or the putts just won't fall, rest assured, there always seems to be an ocean, pool or spa nearby to soothe your frustrations.

Hit 'em straight.

— ***Edward Schmidt, Jr.***

About this guide

In this book I'll introduce you to some of the world's great golf resorts — all of which are located in Florida. In addition, I've highlighted many excellent semiprivate residential, public and military courses.

Florida also has many world-class private courses, yet I do not feature these prominently. Here's why: Many visiting golfers find getting a tee time at one of these gated enclaves more difficult than entrance into the Kremlin. For those intent on playing a private course, I have suggested strategies in Chapter 1, or you can check with your concierge who might have connections.

The book is organized in a predictable sequence that most visitors go through. First, planning the trip, then playing golf, and finally a primer on Florida golf course real estate for those who want to buy a permanent Florida golf getaway.

Many golfers mistakenly view Florida as a homogeneous chunk of land peppered with flat, palm-laden courses. This is an erroneous stereotype. Different regions of the state have distinct personalities in golf course design, topography, climate and lifestyle. Consequently, I have divided the state into six regions, each featuring an overview and a map, which will help you find the region best suited to your golf game and vacation activity preferences.

There also are references and details on meeting and conference facilities for those wanting to mix business with golf. Florida's resorts are recognized as some of the nation's best meeting and convention venues with state-of-the-art meeting facilities to complement their golf offerings.

Men and women do not live by golf alone, and I've included information on attractions such as theme parks, museums and shopping areas located near resorts. There also is information on off-the-course recreation, from tennis to fishing to sailing and everything in between.

To avoid confusion, all references to golf course yardages are from the back tees. I have stayed away from citing room rates because they vary from season to season and the numerous golf packages offered by major resorts discourage paying rack rates.

1

Lodge at Ponte Vedra Beach

Planning a Florida Golf Getaway

All of us who play golf regularly have seen the golfer who, with no practice swing, steps up to the first tee and flails away at his ball, hoping for a 290-yarder straight down the middle of the fairway. The lack of preparation usually results in a world-class shank.

A similar lack of preparation when planning a golf vacation can create disastrous results, too.

Keep in mind that only a few Florida vacation golfers pay over-the-counter hotel rates and greens fees at resorts. Every major Florida golf resort offers packages that combine golf, accommodations and amenities at a discount. The world of golf resort package vacations is a complex one, and those who take the time to examine all the options have a better chance of spending less and playing more.

There are many types of packages at both ends of the price spectrum and almost as many ways of planning a golf vacation. Here are some considerations when planning your Florida golf getaway:

Contacting your resort of choice

Once you've thumbed through this book and been romanced visually by Florida's golf resorts, hopefully you'll narrow your choices to a couple of finalists.

The majority of resorts have a toll-free telephone number, but you should be armed with some knowledge before you pick up the phone and make reservations.

Some of Florida's golf resorts have as many as six golf packages available. Known in the travel industry as "in-house" packages, they usually combine accommodations, golf and other amenities at one price (generally requiring double occupancy, sometimes quad occupancy). Depending on the amenities available at a particular resort, you might find "spa and golf," "tennis and golf," "fitness and golf,"

"instruction and golf" packages as well as other combinations.

For example, one major Southeast Florida resort offers a three-day/two-night golf and fitness package, which includes accommodations, two full breakfasts, daily unlimited greens fees on any of the resort's five courses, complimentary golf bag storage, reserved starting times, three buckets of range balls daily, complimentary daily entrance to the spa's two group fitness classes, a full-body massage and a welcome gift. Obviously, this package is ideal if you are into the spa life. But if you don't know an herbal wrap from a sauna, this package isn't for you. Fortunately, the same resort offers a package for golf traditionalists who want only golf. This package includes all of the above-mentioned features without the spa privileges.

Ask the resort operator to send you information on all golf packages offered, and be sure to tell the operator what time of the year you're planning your vacation.

It's important to find the package suited to your tastes, budget and time constraints. For instance, if you'll be staying at an Orlando-area golf resort and you know you'll be doing a lot of theme-park hopping between rounds, then a standard golf/accommodations would be well-suited to your vacation plan. Prices always are subject to change and vary from season to season, so be sure to confirm the price when you make your reservations.

Once you've decided on a particular resort, it also is a good idea to book your tee times with the pro shop when you make your room reservation. Typically, most resort courses will book tee times 60 to 90 days in advance.

Ideally, you should book your golf getaway three to five months in advance, especially if you plan on visiting peninsular Florida during January, February or March, when the courses are most crowded.

There also are several major Florida resort hotels with no on-site golf courses that offer golf packages. Utilizing golf courses near their properties, hotels such as Peabody Orlando in Orlando, Sonesta Sanibel Harbor Resort in Fort Myers and Edgewater Beach Resort in Naples as well as others throughout the state offer golf/accommodations packages.

Golf packaging specialists

A relatively new phenomenon, golf packaging specialists are favored by golfers who like one-stop shopping. Some golf packaging specialists can package everything from course selection and preferred tee times to hotels, rental cars and air fare. Essentially, these companies are golf travel agencies. No safaris. No honeymoon cruises. No ski trips. These companies concern themselves only with booking golf packages.

Golf packagers actually are wholesale tour operators who, in exchange for booking several rounds of golf at courses and resorts, are offered annually contracted discounts.

One of the nation's largest golf packaging companies, Golfpac, is located in Orlando. The 15-year-old firm has booked more than 100,000 golfers on tours in Florida. Because of its extensive long-term relationships with Florida golf courses and resorts, Golfpac offers packages that are price competitive and often cheaper than the resorts themselves. Also, the golf packaging specialists get price breaks because of volume buying.

Golfpac customers can choose from more than 126 Florida golf courses. The company offers packages at resorts such as Grenelefe, Doral and Palm-Aire Spa Resort as well as accommodations/golf packages that feature play on area courses with accommodations at price competitive non-golf hotels like Embassy Suites, Marriott Residence Inn and Holiday Inn.

For those who want only to play golf, the latter package is appealing because it allows more variety in course selection. You simply select your hotel package and choose from a list of golf courses to play. From your requests, the company arranges and confirms your tee times.

A typical Golfpac package in-cludes accommodations, daily greens fees, confirmed tee times, shared cart (first 18 holes each day), all sales and resort taxes, 24-hour customer service hot line, free detailed map (Orlando, Miami, Tampa, Fort Lauderdale) and free discount coupons to Orlando-area attractions.

Be aware that some courses, especially during the prime winter months, have a surcharge that is added to the package price. A surcharge generally reflects a higher cost of greens fees and cart charge during that time of year.

Another advantage of booking with a golf package specialist is insurance against rainouts. Most resorts do not refund in-house package golfers when a rainout occurs. But golf packaging specialists use a voucher system and are charged only for rounds played. Consequently, if a golfer never gets on the course because of inclement weather, he or she can get a partial refund from the golf packaging specialist if play cannot be relocated to another course.

World of Golf, a golf packaging company based in Apopka (12 miles north of Orlando), specializes in packages in the Central Florida area. It offers packages at more than 30 courses, including major resorts such as Walt Disney World, Mission Inn and Grenelefe.

Typically, a golf packaging company requires a deposit ranging from $50 to $100 per person when confirming reservations. The balance of the package usually is due 21 to 30 days before arrival. During this time period the company will send you hotel and car vouchers (if applicable) and confirmed tee times.

For high-rolling golfers, a Tallahassee company named Regal Retreats packages golf getaways that feature golf outings with PGA Tour professionals at major Florida resorts. Prices range from $2,500 per person to $50,000 per

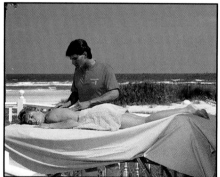

Ponte Vedra Inn & Club

person.

Your best bet is to contact a golf packaging specialist and request a catalog, which has all courses and resorts participating in the program as well as procedures and other information. (See Chapter 10 for addresses and phone numbers of Florida-based golf package specialists.)

Contacting a travel agent

Because of the ever-changing nature of the golf resort package business, agents with a good understanding of Florida and its climate (different parts of the state attract golfers at varying times of the year) are the ones who'll get their clients on the best courses at the best rates. Any agent can phone and book you into a resort with a golf course. The key is to find the resort that has the location, climate, amenities and golf courses that fit your needs.

If you get the impression your agent doesn't know a golf ball from

a tennis ball, find another agent or contact the resorts yourself and do your own research. Unless you have a longstanding relationship with an agent you trust or the agent is knowledgeable about the Florida market and its resorts, you're asking for trouble.

Special packages

Watch for special packages put together by tourism offices or groups of hotels. For instance, the Tampa/Hillsborough Convention and Visitors Association offers a golf package program from June 1 through Dec. 15 that features "stay & play" at Tampa-area courses and hotels. More than a dozen hotels and 11 golf courses participate in the program.

In Northwest Florida, several hotels have joined with hotels on the Alabama coast for the Flori-Bama Golf Holiday Package, which gives golfers a wide selection of courses and hotels.

Tourism officials know that golfers tend to spend as much off the course as on, so these types of packages are becoming more and more popular to attract golfers to particular regions.

Many of these special packages are advertised in major golf publications.

Discount cards

Let's say you're planning an extended Florida golf getaway. Whatever the reason, golfers with few time constraints should investigate "discount" cards, which are money-saving options for those who want to play a different course

each day.

Discount cards come in many forms. The basic premise is that the business or organization issuing the card has reached agreement with numerous courses to provide complimentary or discounted greens fees, while golfers share the rental of the golf cart.

One of the nation's largest programs is The Golf Card, based in Salt Lake City. The Golf Card entitles the cardholder to two 18-hole rounds at each of the 1,750 golf properties across the country and around the world participating in the program. In addition, the Golf Card offers special golf packages at 350 golf resorts.

More than 40 Florida resorts participate in The Golf Card's Stay & Play resort program. Among the participants are Amelia Island Plantation on Amelia Island, Grenelefe Resort in Grenelefe, Saddlebrook in Wesley Chapel and Innisbrook in Tarpon Springs.

The Golf Card costs $75 for a single yearlong membership (or $120 for a husband and wife). Each member receives *The Golf Traveler Atlas* and the bimonthly *Golf Traveler* magazine, which has complete listings of all member golf courses and resorts.

Another popular program is sponsored by *GolfWeek* newspaper in Winter Haven, Fla. Subscribers to the publication receive a VIP card that entitles cardholders to play with no greens fees on more than 50 selected courses throughout the Southeast. Florida resorts participating in the program include Sheraton Palm Coast, Marriott Orlando World Center and Orange Lake Country Club in Kissimmee.

The North Florida PGA Passport card offers free greens fees at more than 80 Florida golf courses between May 1 and Oct. 31. The Ravines in Jacksonville, Saddlebrook in Wesley Chapel and Walt Disney World Resort in Lake Buena Vista are some of the golf resorts participating in the program.

The discount card idea is so popular that some charity organizations have adopted the concept as a fund-raiser. For example, the American Lung Association in Orlando offers the Golf Privilege Card, which features free rounds on more than 270 courses statewide between May 1 and Nov. 1.

Before joining any program, carefully examine the restrictions and number of rounds allowed on participating courses. Most programs require cart rental. For addresses and phone numbers, see listing in Chapter 10.

Private courses

It would be a major oversight not to address play on private Florida golf courses. Nothing can enhance a Florida golf getaway more than playing a round on one of these high-profile courses. To be sure, several are among the state's most expensive to build and highly rated layouts. Courses like Black Diamond Ranch in Lecanto, Seminole in North Palm Beach and Lake Nona and Bay Hill in Orlando rate as some of the nation's best.

Provided your last name isn't Bush or Trump, you'll have to do some planning to have a chance at playing these courses. If you drive up to the front gate unannounced with your clubs in your trunk and a smile on your face, you'll probably receive the standard reception — a suggestion by the not-so-smiling security guard for you to execute a U-turn.

However, almost all private country clubs have reciprocal guest policies of some type with varying restrictions. Most policies fall into one of the following categories:

■ A requirement that you be invited by a member, and that member must accompany you at the club.

■ An invitation by a member but that member does not have to accompany you at the club.

■ You are welcome as a guest as long as you phone in advance and bring credentials to prove that you are an out-of-town private club member.

Most private Florida clubs fall into the first two categories. Don't give up, though. If you really want to play a private course, try having your club pro write or phone, on your behalf, the head pro at the club you wish to visit for an invitation. This is one of the more successful approaches because of the rapport among club professionals.

Golf attire

Most of the courses you will play will be semiprivate or private country clubs, and resort wear is expected on all courses. Golf shoes, socks and shirts with collars are required at all times for men (no cutoffs or sneakers). Shorts are acceptable but must be a minimum of 16 inches in length. For women, golf shoes and socks, shirts, slacks, shorts or skirts are recommended.

Obviously, packing for a golf getaway is personal preference. Some golfers pack enough golf shirts to change hourly, others opt to take along a couple and do laundry in the hotel bathtub. Regardless of your approach, here are a few helpful hints:

■ Be sure to take some stain remover for golf mud. If you don't, you might be bringing home a mud-splotched pair of golf slacks as a souvenir of your trip.

■ Take along an extra pair of golf shoes (with shoe trees) so you have a dry pair available in case you get caught in a downpour.

■ Bring along shoe polish. It's surprising how many golfers wear fashionable slacks and shirt outfits with shoes that look worse than those worn by golf course maintenance workers.

■ Take a windbreaker or rain suit with you. Florida is known for its regular showers, especially in the summer months.

■ Take a golf hat or visor to

Doral Resort & Country Club

protect your face from the sun. Meteorologists estimate the sun shines in Florida two-thirds of the time sunlight is possible.

One more thing. Don't forget your golf clubs.

2

The Breakers

The Resort Course

Golf course designer Ron Garl compares resort courses to flashy sports cars. "It's easy to get overwhelmed by the beauty and power, but you need to take a few spins around the block before you can make a judgment. A resort course is much the same in that you need to play it a few times before casting judgment."

Generally, resort courses tend to be flashier than public courses. Florida's high-profile resort courses resemble the style of the resort hotels for which they have been designed — ornate, expensive with eye-catching design elements. They tend to be strong on cosmetics and glitz.

To be sure, golfers that want flamboyant and fun-to-play features like island greens, Scottish design touches, dimpled fairways and crater bunkers should look first to resort courses.

A cursory glance at Florida's resort courses reveals a wide variety of design features. At the Shera-ton Bonaventure Resort and Spa in Fort Lauderdale one hole is rimmed by a waterfall; The Grand Cypress Resort in Orlando sports the Scottish look; the Sawgrass TPC Stadium Course in Ponte Vedra Beach is noted for its island green on the 17th hole; the Cypress Course at Palm Beach Polo & Country Club in West Palm Beach has church pew bunkers; and Golden Ocala in Ocala has eight replica holes, including the 12th and 13th at Augusta National.

Tom Fazio

"I don't think features themselves necessarily make a resort course more difficult," says Tom Fazio, a golf course designer from Jupiter, Fla. "The placement of hazards such as trees, bunkers and water makes a course difficult. Golf is a game of angles, and it's a designer's job to make the angles playable for the high-handicapper, who generally dominates resort courses, yet challenging for the scratch golfer."

Fazio has designed Florida resort courses such as Long Point at Amelia Island and Bluewater Bay in Niceville, as well as what many golf aficionados consider the quintessential resort course, the oceanside Wild Dunes layout near Charleston, S.C.

Garl, a golf course architect based in Lakeland, Fla., has more than 125 designs to his credit, including Florida resort courses Grenelefe South in Grenelefe and the Dunes Course at Palm Beach Polo & Country Club in West Palm Beach.

Ron Garl

Garl suggests golfers should approach resort courses this way: "They often get more publicity than other courses — whether they deserve it or not — because of the resort's corporate advertising muscle. Thus, it's easier to get a reputation and 'name' value. Most weekend golfers tend to get intimidated by 'name' courses. Yet, golfers should keep in mind the resort would like nothing better than to have them as a repeat guest. If the resort course is too penal and not fun to play, chances are some of the guests don't return.

"As a general rule, the degree of difficulty on a resort course rises as you play more holes. That way golfers have a better chance of feeling good at the beginning of a round and they can build some confidence."

Bill Amick

Resort courses are, for the most part, visually spectacular, which alters golfers' perceptions. "On many resort courses, if you look closely," says Bill Amick, a Daytona Beach golf course designer, "water is used for visual appeal as much as a hazard. Greens also tend to be larger and flatter on resort courses."

Amick, who started designing courses in Florida in 1959, has designed more than 80 golf courses,

Sheraton Bonaventure Resort and Spa

21

including resort layouts at Perdido Bay in Pensacola and Killearn Country Club & Inn in Tallahassee.

Actually, there are few pure resort courses in Florida, explains Fazio. Many resort courses have resident exposure, and many housing development courses are designed with more flair and visual appeal.

Two of Fazio's most famous Florida designs — Black Diamond Ranch in Lecanto with its quarry holes and heavily wooded Lake Nona in Orlando — are located at private residential developments, yet easily could be at resorts because of their astounding visual appeal and playability.

Most assuredly, there are exceptions to the "resort courses are fun to play" adage. Just ask some of the dejected souls who have been brought to their knees by difficult courses like Pete Dye's often vilified TPC Stadium at Sawgrass Course or Dick Wilson's Doral "Blue Monster" in Miami.

However, any golfer worth his putter will tell you that golf enjoyment comes in many forms, and at extremely tough courses the fun is in the challenge.

"At least after playing a challenging resort course, the golfer can soothe his worries at the hotel pool or spa. That sure beats having to go back to work the next morning," quips Garl.

Adjusting your stroke

Once you step onto a Florida golf course, the object of the game is the same as anywhere — beat par if you're a low-handicapper or don't lose too many balls if you're a

Mission Inn

high-handicapper. There are, however, a few things golfers of all levels need to know before playing a Florida golf course.

First, most Florida courses are planted with Bermuda grass, which mats differently from the bent and blue grasses used in the North. Bermuda grass makes for more difficult hitting, especially in the rough and on greens, because the ball nestles deeper in the grass.

"The Bermuda roughs in Florida will make what look like easy shots difficult ones," Garl says. "The collars around the green can be

tricky, too."

Following a Florida tournament a few years ago, a bewildered Mark McCumber, a Jacksonville resident, remarked to a reporter, "There's not a rye-grass rough in the world I can't hit a ball out of, but the Bermuda roughs in Florida can sometimes make it just about impossible."

Bermuda grass makes for a deceptive and slower putting surface. Randy Cahall, director of golf for Grenelefe Resort, explains how to read Bermuda greens: "If the portion of the green you're putting on is darker than the rest, the grass is lying toward you, and you can expect more break. If the grass is much lighter in color you're putting with the grain and you'll get less break."

Bermuda grass does have an advantage in the winter. It lies dormant in cold months and is seeded with different types of "cool grasses" that flourish in chilly temperatures. The result is verdant, carpetlike fairways that make the courses visually appealing.

For those golfers who have a habit of playing "on the beach," the sand in Florida traps is different, too. Generally, it is much fluffier than that on northern courses. Golfers need to use more force when hitting out of Florida sand, says Cahall.

If you're like Lee Trevino and you grew up in West Texas playing windswept courses, your game may be well-suited for Florida courses in the winter. The constantly changing wind in Florida can affect from one day to the next the way you approach the same hole.

During the winter, especially at seaside areas, the wind blows an average of 20-25 mph from all directions. It may blow from the north one day, the northeast the following day, the east the next, and so on. Oftentimes, what seemed like an easy course the

Amelia Island Plantation

first day can turn into a monster if the wind direction changes.

The first time around

It's a common scenario at resorts and golf clubs in Florida — a visitor who never has played the course proudly informs playing partners of his handicap and shot-making abilities on his "home" course. A few holes into the round, the visitor's playing partners don't know whether to laugh or cry at the visitor's futile effort. The visi-

tor can't seem to find the fairway. The visitor chops at the ball like a lumberjack. Every recovery shot turns into a disaster. Truth is, if a golfer doesn't take the time to prepare when playing a golf course for the first time the experience can be an agonizing four or five hours.

Because Florida has such a large number of resort and new residential courses, chances are golfers will find themselves at the first tee of a layout they've never seen or played before.

Here are 10 tips to help keep your score low and your spirits high:

■ Ask for a yardage guide. Most major resorts and upscale residential golf clubs have golf guides that offer a hole-by-hole description of the course or courses. "Even if you're not playing until the following day, it's a

Grand Cypress Resort

good idea to drop by the clubhouse and pick one up," says Cahall. "You'll build up a little confidence for the next day just by knowing the basic layout of the course."

■ Ask the pro about hazards and types of lies. The pro can inform golfers on the height and type of rough, hilly terrain that makes for problem lies, and where the most difficult hazards are located. "Looking at a course guide doesn't always give you the full picture of the difficulty of a course," says Jim Muszak, director of golf at Mission Inn Golf & Ten-

nis Resort in Howey-in-the-Hills. "A short conversation with the pro or assistant pro can sometimes shave a couple strokes off your game just because you'll know what hazards have caused the most trouble for other golfers."

■ Practice before your round. It's probably the most amazing phenomenon in golf. High-handicappers, who boom banana balls into water hazards and swing at balls in the rough like a worker with a machete, bypass all the low-handicappers at the practice range and head straight for the first tee.

Paul Celano, director of golf at the Grand Cypress Resort, says guests often are so eager to play the course they've heard so much about that they forego practicing. "That's a major mistake," says Celano. "I can understand the excitement level, but it's imperative a golfer hit a few practice balls before playing."

Celano concedes that most low-handicappers understand the importance of the practice range. He offers this advice for the weekend golfer: "Loosen up with some minor stretching and several practice swings. Then hit about 30 to 35 balls starting with the shorter irons, preferably the [pitching] wedge or sand wedge. You'll be able to tell what type of shot you have that day — a hook or a slice. That's important because if you don't play a lot, your shot won't always be the same. You can use that to your advantage on the course because you'll have a little better idea of where the ball will be going. Also, don't forget to stroke a few putts to get an idea of how fast the greens are."

■ Drive straight rather than long off the tee. A conservative approach off the tee, especially on the first few holes, can do wonders for your confidence. You may know where the hazards are by consulting a golf guide, however, if you boom one and don't carry a fairway bunker or water hazard, it could set the tone for the rest of the round. Get into the flow with some straight shots, then progress to your big swing.

■ Use enough club. Cahall has seen thousands of golfers playing Grenelefe's three courses, and he has noticed one glaring problem with weekend golfers. "From what I've seen, they just don't use enough club. As a general rule, they should use one more club than they think they need," suggests Cahall.

■ Think a shot or two ahead. One of the most common mistakes golfers make on courses they've never played, points out Celano, is they worry so much about their tee shot they don't concern themselves with a total strategy to play the hole.

"A golfer should visualize one or two shots ahead. It sounds obvious,

but it's not easy to do. For example, if you've got a crowd with all eyes on you at the tee, most people are just praying to strike the ball cleanly much less what they'll do after the shot. That's where you have to concentrate and be prepared mentally," advises Celano.

■ Don't try miracle shots. If you're a high-handicapper, think of bogey as par. The conservative approach will be reflected in your overall score. "Trying miracle shots is where most high-handicappers get into trouble," says Celano. "They make a bad shot then try to emulate Seve Ballesteros, the recovery shot master, and hit an almost impossible shot in the hole.

Doral Resort and Country Club

If a golfer realizes his or her limitations, the results will be much better."

■ Shoot for the middle of the green. For the weekend golfer aiming at the pin puts additional pressure on approach shots. Just get on the green first, then maybe

you can gamble on sinking a long putt instead of a safe lag. There's not a better feeling in golf than seeing your ball safely on the green while your partner takes the cart to chase down his errant shot.

■ Take your time. Admittedly, most of Florida's golf courses are crowded during the winter. There is a tendency to speed up your swing in hopes of speeding up play as a form of respect to the groups playing behind you. There is no reason to treat every shot as if you were qualifying for the U.S. Open; however, you should take a deep breath and a practice stroke or two before addressing your ball.

■ Enjoy yourself. Just remember you're at a golf course in Florida. Millions of golfers would love to be in your shoes. So you splash a few, hit some "fat" shots and shank a drive or two. You're not at work so you won't be docked any salary. Golf is supposed to be play, not work. Have fun!

3
Northwest Florida

Overview

Though the majority of Florida's visiting golfers roam the fairways of the state's more celebrated courses, few would be disappointed with the offerings in Northwest Florida — often called the Panhandle.

There are more than 400 holes of golf in this region, ranging in character from seaside courses framed by the sugar-white sands and aquamarine waters of the Gulf of Mexico to lagoon and marsh-laden layouts to heavily wooded courses with elevation changes in the interior.

Generally, Northwest Florida is full of contrasts much like its golf courses. Though its larger cities, Tallahassee and Pensacola, and beach towns reflect a Sunbelt cosmopolitan air, the region is predominantly rural.

The Panhandle, for the most part, is a little old-fashioned and moves at a pace slower than the rest of the state.

Tallahassee, Florida's capital city situated where the Panhandle meets the peninsula, is a jewel of old mansions, modern office buildings, sparkling lakes, moss-draped trees, flower-filled parks and golf courses ablaze with roses and azaleas.

Pensacola, anchoring the western end of the Panhandle on the Gulf, is renowned for its white sand beaches (99 percent quartz) and historical district.

Major beach towns, which include Panama City, Destin and Fort Walton Beach have some of the longest stretches of unspoiled beach in Florida. For years, Southerners have been coming to the

Bluewater Bay

beaches in droves. In fact, so many Southerners from Georgia and Alabama own summer retreats or have standing reservations at hotels along the Emerald Coast — an area stretching from Pensacola to Panama City — that the coast has been dubbed the "Redneck Riviera."

Recently, though, many Northerners and Canadians have discovered the uncrowded and unspoiled region, and the area steadily is shedding its dubious nickname.

Northwest Florida also attracts many active and retired military tourists and golfers who take advantage of the recreational facilities provided at the area's military installations. The region is home to 14 of the state's 34 military bases.

Without Florida's year-round typical tropical climate — November through February temperatures sometimes dip to the 30s and 40s — the Panhandle often is ignored by Florida travel literature. Yet, the region's golf courses are playable every day of the year, and the average high temperature from January to March is 67 degrees.

During the winter months, a sweater and windbreaker generally provide adequate protection against the chilly winds.

Not surprisingly, when the tem-

perature drops in the Panhandle, so do hotel rates and greens fees. From September through May, the region features some of the state's most competitive golf/accommodations packages.

During the summer, when it occasionally seems as if every golfer south of the Mason-Dixon line is grappling for a tee time, the rates are higher but still cheaper than peninsular Florida.

Thanks to a building boom that started in the mid-1970s and has continued at a bustling pace, the Emerald Coast has numerous first-class resort hotels, real estate/resort communities, condominium towers, restaurants and championship golf courses.

Off-the-course recreation revolves around water sports such as fishing, sailing, snorkeling and scuba diving in the coastal region. Camping, hiking and sightseeing are big in the interior.

Because the waters off the coasts of Panama City, Pensacola, Fort Walton Beach and Destin are considered some of the nation's most fertile fishing grounds, more than a few golfers also bring their rods and reels and combine a deep-sea fishing excursion with a golf getaway.

Northwest Florida is accessible by air with daily commercial flights into all of the region's major cities.

A car is almost a necessity on most air visits, especially if you're planning on playing more than the course or courses located at your particular resort. Shuttle vans providing transportation to and from resorts are not as prevalent as in the southern reaches of the state.

Killearn Country Club & Inn
Tallahassee

The Killearn's three nine-hole tracks retain all the lushness of their former life as dairy farm land. Not many palm trees here.

The course, designed by golf course architect Bill Amick and built in 1964, includes majestic oaks, pines, gently rolling hills and subtle valleys.

All three nines play to par 36. The South is 3,532 yards; East 3,493 yards; and North 3,367 yards. Says Amick: "I had lots of design freedom and I fit the holes to the very attractive rolling land, utilizing the contours and groups of huge oak trees to dogleg certain holes. We moved very few trees, which give the course a park-like feel."

When playing the East/South combination, golfers can build up their confidence early as the course is relatively easy the first few holes. There is a variety of elevated tees and greens as well as strategically placed lakes and sand traps.

Killearn's staff is headed by golf director Becky Sauers, LPGA golf professional. Group and individual instruction is available.

The 39-room Killearn Inn features a unique concept of Execu-

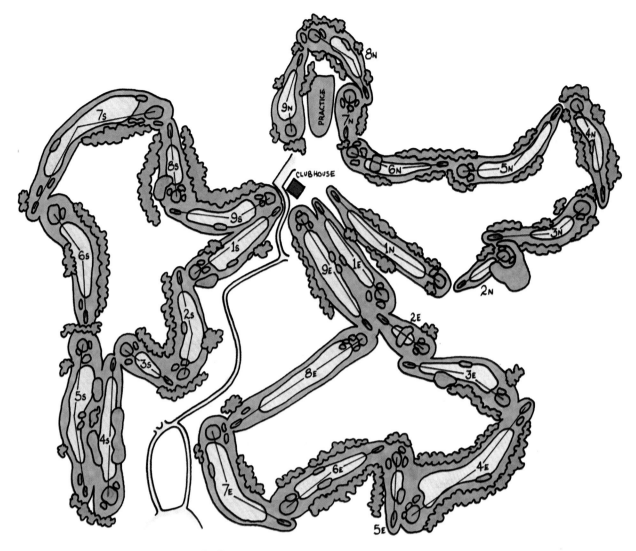

South Course

Hole	1	2	3	4	5	6	7	8	9
Yards	391	378	178	467	506	437	570	223	382
Par	4	4	3	4	5	4	5	3	4

Yardage: 3,532; Par: 36

East Course

Hole	1	2	3	4	5	6	7	8	9
Yards	394	179	362	525	218	395	465	511	444
Par	4	3	4	5	3	4	4	5	4

Yardage: 3,493; Par: 36

North Course

Hole	1	2	3	4	5	6	7	8	9
Yards	574	200	377	349	508	385	170	405	399
Par	5	3	4	4	5	4	3	4	4

Yardage: 3,367; Par: 36

tive Suites with adjoining individual or multiple rooms.

For tennis lovers, the resort offers four lighted hard courts and four clay courts. Other sources of recreation include racquetball and handball courts, an Olympic-size swimming pool, fitness center and miles of surrounding roads for jogging.

The golf complex is situated within Killearn Estates, a residential development that encompasses 3,500 acres.

Address: 100 Tryon Circle, Tallahassee, Fla. 32308
Phone: (904) 893-2186
No. of rooms: 39
No. of holes: 27
Sports facilities: tennis, fitness center, pool and jogging trails
Restaurants: 2
Business facilities: 7,000 square feet of meeting space, six meeting rooms can accommodate groups 10 to 100
Location: Tallahassee
Nearby attractions: Calhoun Street Historical District, Museum of Florida History, Maclay Gardens State Park and Wakulla Springs State Park

Perdido Bay Resort
Pensacola

Home of the PGA Pensacola Open from 1978 through 1987, Perdido Bay long has been recognized as one of Florida's most challenging courses. The 7,154-yard, par-72 Bill Amick design places a premium on driving accuracy.

Rest assured, if you're spraying balls left and right off the tee, your score will add up quicker than points at an NBA game.

Case in point: One of the PGA Tour's perennial leaders in driving accuracy is Curtis Strange, who just happens to own the Perdido Bay course record of 62.

Numerous water hazards, tricky greens and trees that always seem to be in the line of approach shots make the course a true test of your shotmaking skills. The par-5, 502-yard 11th hole requires a tee shot down the middle of the fairway or you'll be pulling out the ball retriever.

Both sides of the fairway are lined with water, and a small lake fronts the green.

The 2,200-acre resort offers several golf package options. Golfers can arrange to stay at nearby hotels such as the Perdido Beach Hilton, Comfort Inn on Perdido Key and Hospitality Inn, which have golf privilege agreements with the resort, or at Cottage on the Green villas that overlook the course.

"Life is a beach" at Perdido Bay, as most of the non-golfing activities revolve around activities on the Gulf of Mexico and its beaches. Swimming, snorkeling, sailing, windsurfing and sport fishing are among the most popular water sports.

Perdido Bay also features an equestrian center and shopping area. Sunset watching is a popular pastime at the resort's two lounges, and more nightlife is available in Pensacola, a 20-minute drive from the resort.

Address: 1 Doug Ford Drive, Pensacola, Fla. 32507
Phone: (800) 874-5355, in Florida (904) 492-1213
No. of rooms: 20
No. of holes: 18
Sports facilities: tennis, pool and hot tub
Restaurants: 1
Business facilities: Limited business facilities are available
Location: Pensacola area
Nearby attractions: North Hill Historic District, Naval Aviation Museum, Seville Square and deep-sea fishing

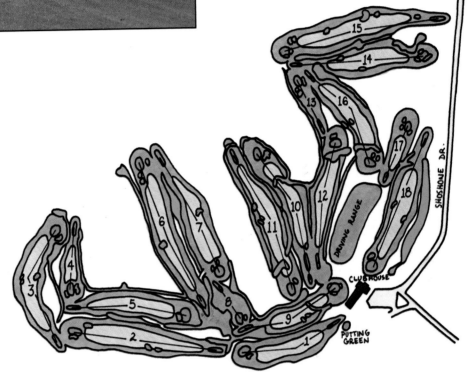

Perdido Bay

Hole	1	2	3	4	5	6	7	8	9	10	11	12	13	14	15	16	17	18
Yards	379	560	419	210	411	538	445	173	373	447	502	422	236	441	560	390	194	454
Par	4	5	4	3	4	5	4	3	4	4	5	4	3	4	5	4	3	4

Yardage: 7,154; Par: 72

Sandestin Resort
Destin

When golfers think of great seaside courses, Pebble Beach in California and "The Teeth of the Dog" in the Dominican Republic come to mind. One of Florida's great seaside layouts is the Links at Sandestin, a 2,600-acre resort on the Gulf of Mexico and the Choctawhatchee Bay.

The par-72, 6,676-yard Links Course has 13 holes where water comes into play, including five that border the bay. The fourth hole, a relatively short par 5 at 501 yards, is reputedly one of the toughest holes in Florida because the narrow fairway is flanked by a lagoon on the left and the Choctawhatchee marsh on the right from tee to green. Though

the Links can be demanding, high handicappers need not shake in their golf shoes because the gener-

Linkside Course

Hole	1	2	3	4	5	6	7	8	9	10	11	12	13	14	15	16	17	18
Yards	425	537	171	501	342	415	161	343	431	513	356	195	419	198	417	370	354	528
Par	4	5	3	5	4	4	3	4	4	5	4	3	4	3	4	4	4	5

Yardage: 6,676; Par: 72

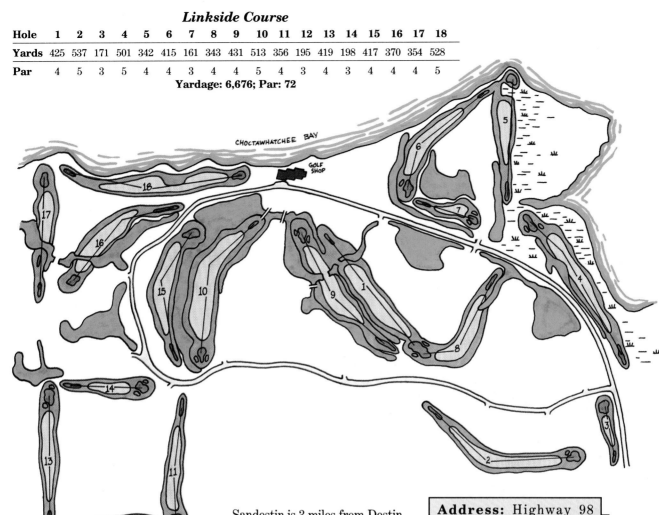

ous tee positions allow them still to have fun.

Sandestin's other 18-hole course, the Baytowne, also plays to a par 72, measuring 6,796 yards. The Baytowne layout recently added nine more holes. The Baytowne is considered easier than the Links course because of its wider fairways and fewer water hazards.

The fifth hole on the Baytowne course epitomizes the beauty of this region of the state. The tee on the 366-yard, par-4 hole, perched atop a 40-foot-high sand dune, rewards golfers with an eye-popping view of tropical green Gulf waters.

Both of Sandestin's courses were designed by veteran architect Tom Jackson. Each course has its own pro shop. The resort's professional staff also offers individual lessons and group clinics.

Sandestin is 3 miles from Destin, a resort midway between Pensacola and Panama City, renowned for its fishing.

If you want to combine a golf getaway with a world-class, deep-sea fishing excursion, this resort is one that can accommodate both requests. Sandestin is located minutes from Kelly Docks, where 125 deep-sea fishing charter boats sail daily. Destin boasts the title "Sport Fishing Capital of the Gulf," and with good reason — more billfish are brought into Destin each year than all other Gulf fishing ports combined.

Every water sport imaginable is offered at Sandestin as well as tennis on hard, clay and grass surfaces, a fitness center and many other activities.

Guests can select from a wide range of accommodations including private villas, waterfront condominiums and patio homes. For bargain hunters, Sandestin has spring, fall and winter packages.

Address: Highway 98 East, Destin, Fla. 32541-4199
Phone: (800) 277-0800, (904) 267-8150
No. of rooms: 525
No. of holes: 45
Sports facilities: tennis, pools, bicycle paths, fitness center, jet ski and sail boat rentals and deep-sea fishing charters
Restaurants: 5
Business facilities: 17,000 square feet of meeting space. The conference center overlooks Choctawhatchee Bay
Location: Fort Walton Beach area
Nearby attractions: on-site shopping featuring 30 specialty shops, Seaside, a village of Victorian-style homes with large verandas, tin roofs and gazebos 15 miles east of Destin

Marriott's Bay Point Resort
Panama City

Following an arduous round, Stan Mikita, former star of the NHL's Chicago Black Hawks, had this whimsical assessment of the much-talked-about Bay Point Lagoon Legend course:

"I knew Bay Point was on the Gulf, but I didn't plan to be in the water the whole time I was playing golf."

Water comes into play on 16 holes of the 6,942-yard, par-72 course that was designed by Bruce Devlin and Bob Von Hagge.

Home of the PGA Tour Qualifying School, the Lagoon Legend was selected as the "best new golf course in America" by *Playboy* magazine in 1986. An intimidating slope rating of 152, the highest in Florida, will force golfers to use every club in their bag.

Honestly, this is not a beginner's course, but low and high handicappers alike can regale in the pristine surroundings — lush tropical foliage, sugar-white sand dunes, carpetlike Bermuda grass fairways and Penncross bent grass greens.

The par-4, 382-yard 18th hole will leave a lasting impression of this layout. You shoot over a lagoon to an island and back over the water to the green.

For golfers whose confidence has been destroyed by the perils of the Lagoon Legend, the resort's other course, The Meadows, with its wide fairways, is a bit easier. Measuring 6,913 yards

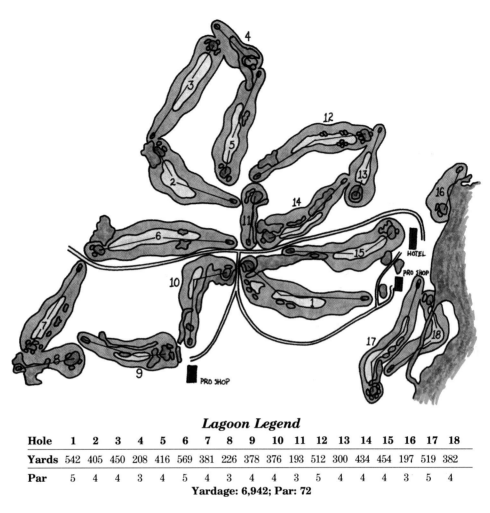

Lagoon Legend

Hole	1	2	3	4	5	6	7	8	9	10	11	12	13	14	15	16	17	18
Yards	542	405	450	208	416	569	381	226	378	376	193	512	300	434	454	197	519	382
Par	5	4	4	3	4	5	4	3	4	4	3	5	4	4	4	3	5	4

Yardage: 6,942; Par: 72

and playing to par 72, The Meadows was designed by Willard Byrd. It also has a memorable finishing hole, a tricky dogleg right with five sand traps and a lake to the right of the green.

The golf complex features two practice putting greens, a driving range, two clubhouses, "Stroke of the Day" complimentary clinics and private golf instruction.

Overlooking St. Andrews Bay, Marriott's Bay Point Resort reigns as the area's most luxurious resort. Guests can select from rooms in the 200-room, pink-stucco, Bermuda-styled hotel, 30 one- and two-bedroom bayfront villas and 155 one- and two-bedroom lake and fairway suites.

Besides golf, there is swimming, tennis (12 clay courts), a 145-boat slip on-site marina, health club, and biking and nature trails.

When planning a trip to Bay Point, fishing and boating enthusiasts might want to schedule around these two major events: the Bay Point Billfish Invitational, a deep-sea fishing tournament with the largest purse ($350,000) in the continental United States, held in July; and the Off-Shore 100, an American Power Boat Association point race held each April on Panama City Beach.

Address: 100 Delwood Beach Road, Panama City Beach, Fla. 32411-7207
Phone: (904) 234-3307, (800) 874-7105
No. of rooms: 385
No. of holes: 36
Sports facilities: tennis, health club, water sports equipment rental, deep-sea fishing charters
Restaurants: 7
Business facilities: 25,000 square feet of space
Location: Panama City area
Nearby attractions: Miracle Strip Amusement Park, Gulf World marine life show

Bluewater Bay
Niceville

You get the feeling Tarzan would enjoy Bluewater Bay's 27-hole layout. The sometimes junglelike course is wooded with pine, oak and magnolia trees and enhanced by marsh and water.

Course designers Tom Fazio and PGA Tour pro Jerry Pate took full advantage of Northern Florida's natural elements — dense tree cover, rolling terrain, sandy soil and a magnificent view of Choctawhatchee Bay.

This is golf at its most challenging and aesthetically pleasing. All three nines are par 36. The Bay nine measures 3,323 yards; Lake 3,485 yards; and Marsh 3,403 yards.

Bluewater Bay sprawls along 1,800 acres on the shores of Choctawhatchee Bay, 18 miles northeast of Fort Walton Beach. It is a secluded and amenity-rich residential-resort community.

Off the links, swimming, sailing and tennis (21 courts) head a long list of activities. The resort also has a 120-boat slip marina. For those who want to drop a line for an hour or so, the bay is an excellent spot to catch bass.

Despite Bluewater Bay's secluded location, visitors do not have to travel great distances for good food. In fact, they need not travel at all. Situated on resort property are three restaurants — Ristorante La Fontana, overlooking the Marina, which offers Northern Italian cuisine; The Greenhouse, an informal eatery at the Golf Clubhouse; and The Heidelberg Haus, a replica of a German Gasthaus restaurant, serving authentic native dishes.

The resort is a favorite destination for active and retired military

Bay Course

Hole	Yards	Par
1	350	4
2	380	4
3	415	4
4	148	3
5	530	5
6	370	4
7	555	5
8	165	3
9	410	4
	3,323	**36**

Lake Course

Hole	Yards	Par
1	380	4
2	515	5
3	420	4
4	180	3
5	425	4
6	465	4
7	195	3
8	385	4
9	520	5
	3,485	**36**

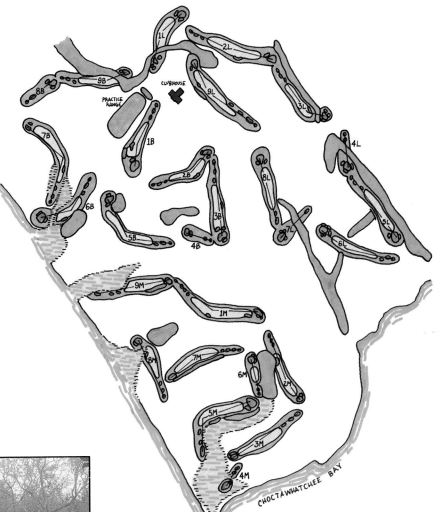

Marsh Course

Hole	Yards	Par
1	529	5
2	410	4
3	435	4
4	142	3
5	555	5
6	164	3
7	420	4
8	319	4
9	429	4
	3,403	**36**

visitors who take advantage of the numerous amenities (including golf) at Eglin Air Force Base, one of the nation's largest bases, which is located 10 miles from Bluewater Bay.

Accommodations at Bluewater Bay include hotel-type rooms, townhouse condominiums, patio homes and golf villas.

Address: P.O. Box 247, Niceville, Fla. 32578-0247
Phone: (800) 874-2128, (904) 897-3613
No. of rooms: 230
No. of holes: 27
Sports facilities: tennis, pools, bicycle paths
Restaurants: 3

Business facilities: 4,000-square-foot conference center can accommodate groups up to 120 people
Location: Fort Walton Beach area
Nearby attractions: on-site boutique shopping, beach 15 miles away and deep-sea fishing

Best Of The Rest

One of the more talked-about Northwest Florida courses is at Shalimar Pointe Golf & Country Club near Fort Walton Beach. Designed by veteran architects Joe Finger and Pete Dye, the 6,760-yard, par-72 course borders the Choctawhatchee Bay and winds gracefully through white sand dunes and tall pines.

Nearby, the Eglin Air Force Base Golf Club features 36 holes and is recognized as one of the finest military golf facilities in the nation.

In Gulf Breeze, a small community east of Pensacola, the 36-hole Tiger Point Golf & Country Club layout is the perfect combination of beauty and challenge.

U.S. Open champion Jerry Pate built and designed the courses, which feature many greens framed by high "spectator" mounds.

The Hombre Golf Club in Panama City Beach is the region's newest course (opened November 1989) and a top-notch challenge. The 7,016-yard, par-72 course is the site of the Ben Hogan Panama City Beach Golf Classic.

Shalimar Pointe Golf & Country Club (semiprivate)
2 Country Club Drive
Shalimar, Fla. 32579
(904) 651-1416
18 holes

Eglin Air Force Base Golf Club (military I.D. required)
Building 1533 Country Club Drive
Niceville, Fla. 32578
(904) 882-2949
36 holes

Tiger Point Golf & Country Club (semiprivate)
1255 Country Club Road
Gulf Breeze, Fla. 32561
(904) 932-1330
36 holes

The Hombre Golf Club (semiprivate)
120 Coyote Pass
Panama City Beach, Fla. 32407
(904) 234-3673
18 holes

Other Courses To Consider

Indian Bayou Golf & Country Club (semiprivate)
P.O Box 306
Destin, Fla. 32541
(904) 837-6192
18 holes

Majette Dunes Golf & Country Club (semiprivate)
5304 Majette Tower Road
Panama City, Fla. 32405
(904) 769-4740
18 holes

Seascape Resort
100 Seascape Ave.
Destin, Fla. 32541
(904) 837-9181
18 holes

Seminole Golf Club (public)
2550 Pottsdamer Road
Tallahassee, Fla. 32304
(904) 644-2582
18 holes

Shoal River Golf & Country Club (semiprivate)
1104 Shoal River Drive
Crestview, Fla. 32536
(904) 682-9065
18 holes

The Club at Hidden Creek (semiprivate)
3070 PGA Blvd.
Gulf Breeze, Fla. 32561
(904) 939-4604
18 holes

Northeast Florida

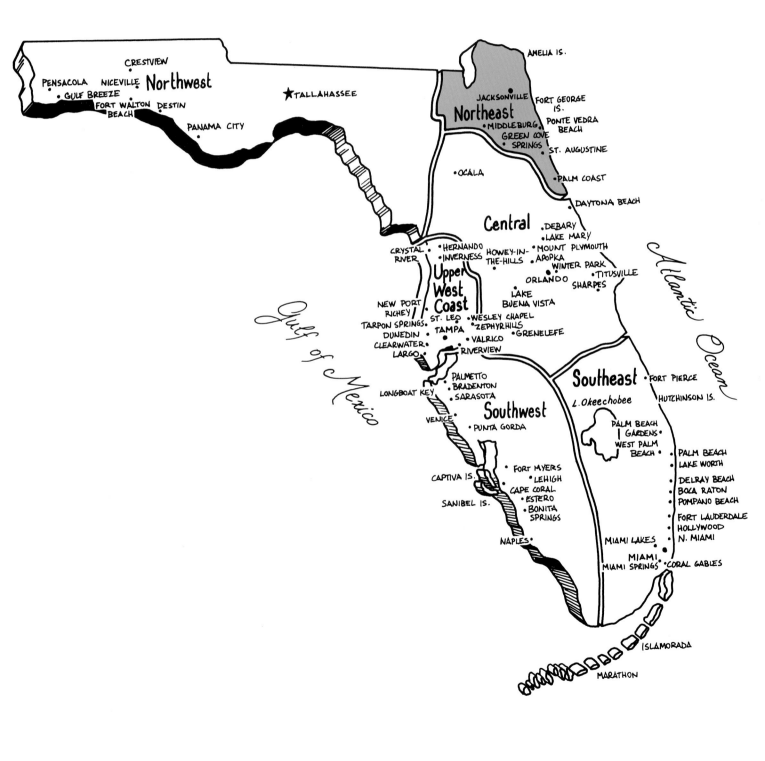

CRESTVIEW
PENSACOLA NICEVILLE Northwest
• GULF BREEZE
FORT WALTON DESTIN
BEACH
PANAMA CITY

★ TALLAHASSEE

AMELIA IS.

JACKSONVILLE FORT GEORGE
Northeast IS.
• MIDDLEBURG PONTE VEDRA
GREEN COVE BEACH
SPRINGS • ST. AUGUSTINE

• OCALA • PALM COAST

DAYTONA BEACH

Central • DEBARY
• LAKE MARY
• HERNANDO • MOUNT PLYMOUTH
CRYSTAL • INVERNESS HOWEY-IN- APOPKA
RIVER THE-HILLS • WINTER PARK
ORLANDO • TITUSVILLE
Upper • SHARPES
West LAKE
NEW PORT Coast BUENA VISTA
RICHEY
TARPON SPRINGS ST. LEO WESLEY CHAPEL
DUNEDIN • ZEPHYRHILLS
CLEARWATER TAMPA • GRENELEFE
LARGO • VALRICO
RIVERVIEW

Gulf of Mexico

Atlantic Ocean

PALMETTO Southeast • FORT PIERCE
BRADENTON
LONGBOAT KEY • SARASOTA L. Okeechobee HUTCHINSON IS.

Southwest
VENICE
• PUNTA GORDA PALM BEACH
GARDENS •
WEST PALM
BEACH • PALM BEACH
• LAKE WORTH
FORT MYERS
CAPTIVA IS. • LEHIGH • DELRAY BEACH
CAPE CORAL • BOCA RATON
• ESTERO • POMPANO BEACH
SANIBEL IS. • BONITA
SPRINGS • FORT LAUDERDALE
• HOLLYWOOD
MIAMI LAKES • N. MIAMI
NAPLES •
MIAMI
MIAMI SPRINGS •CORAL GABLES

ISLAMORADA

MARATHON

Overview

Many people don't even bother to slow down as they motor down Interstate 95 through this region in their efforts to leave the Snowbelt behind.

What are they missing? Great golf, that's what.

The topography of the region lends itself to a variety of course designs, and some of the industry's most respected course architects have designed award-winning layouts here.

Golfers have a veritable smorgasbord of challenging and picturesque courses from which to choose, including courses on semi-tropical barrier islands, seaside layouts and flat, open tracks.

Inland areas offer courses with uncharacteristic hilly terrain. To be sure, the most popular Northeast Florida type of layout features ingredients such as marsh, sand dunes, pine and moss-draped oaks. Even though the land is predominantly flat, designers have used innovative shaping and sculpting techniques to provide aesthetic beauty and difficulty to many courses.

Northeast Florida is more closely allied geographically and culturally with Atlanta than it is with Orlando or Miami. It is characterized by live oaks, antebellum homes and Southern drawls rather than by palm trees, theme parks and Spanish ambience.

Jacksonville, a metropolis sprawling over 840 square miles, is, in land area, America's largest city. It has lifted itself from the municipal decay of the 1960s to emerge as a booming Sunbelt city of the '90s. There are more than 40 golf courses within the city limits.

Less than a 30-minute drive from downtown Jacksonville, Ponte Vedra Beach is one of the nation's most heralded golf meccas. Often described as "Florida's answer to Pebble Beach," Ponte Vedra Beach is a magnificent resort area brimming with championship layouts sporting enviable designer labels such as Pete Dye, Robert Trent Jones, Sr. and Joe Lee.

Golf Digest writer Dan Jenkins once compared Ponte Vedra Beach with Pebble Beach this way: "We have seasons in Ponte Vedra. We get a buffet of weather. There are lots of times when you can play golf by day and burn logs by night. I like that. You want year-round sunshine, go to Bora Bora. We have our famous layout, just like Pebble . . . "

Golf is king in this community. Several of Florida's premier golf resorts are here. In addition, the PGA Tour's national headquarters is located in Ponte Vedra Beach.

Farther south, St. Augustine is the oldest city in the United States. The city was founded by the Spanish who fell in love with the healthy vegetation, agreeable weather and coastline, the same

Hammock Dunes

Marriott at Sawgrass

ingredients that make golf in the area such a pleasure.

Palm Coast, a 20-minute drive south of St. Augustine, is a 42,000-acre residential/resort community featuring four golf courses designed by Arnold Palmer, Bill Amick and Tom Fazio.

Though winters tend to run cooler than in the more southern regions of the state, summers are predictably Florida — hot and muggy. The average high temperature for July to September is 88 degrees. It's a good idea to bring a suitcase full of 100% cotton golf wear, which will help keep you dry and cool on the course.

Winters, as Jenkins suggests, may indeed have you putting logs on the fire. Rest assured, if you don't bring a sweater or two during the winter months, you might be spending all your time by the fire in the clubhouse waving bye-bye to all your well-bundled golf

companions. Frosty winds blowing off the Atlantic have sent more than a few short-sleeved golfers back to the locker room.

The best time for low hotel rates, equally low greens fees and reasonably uncrowded courses is during the fall. The morning air is crisp; the afternoons are of the Indian summer variety, and the humidity is only a faint memory. Playing golf in Northeast Florida this time of year is paradise on earth for golfers.

Once the clubs have been put away for the day, there is much to see and do.

Jacksonville offers a myriad of shopping and dining options. St. Augustine, a city that can be toured on foot, is bursting with historical attractions. The wide, sandy beaches make swimming, surf-casting and boating popular activities. Deep-sea fishing in the Atlantic also is a great way to

spend a day away from the links, and most area resorts can make arrangements on site.

Golfers who also enjoy football can experience the best of both worlds on New Year's Day, when the Mazda Gator Bowl is held in Jacksonville.

Come bowl time, there always is a festive atmosphere at Jacksonville area golf courses, and it's a great time to make friends and talk football.

Access to the region centers on Jacksonville International Airport, situated 30 minutes from the Ponte Vedra Beach area, and served by nine major and three regional carriers. For those driving, Interstate 95, the major artery used by Northerners traveling to the Sunshine State, goes through the Jacksonville, St. Augustine and Palm Coast areas. Even if you're heading farther south, slow down and pull off for a day or two of golf.

Ponte Vedra Inn & Club
Ponte Vedra Beach

When you enter the Ponte Vedra Inn & Club, the Ivy League flavor is unmistakable. In 1937, this venerable oceanside club, 20 miles south of Jacksonville, was seeking members. Jim Stockton, one of its planners and a 1916 Princeton graduate, put out a call to his former classmates. A large number responded, and the club quickly became one of Florida's most sophisticated resorts.

The resort's main lodge, with its large fireplaces and opulent furnishings, provides a cozy atmosphere ideal for post-golf libations and conversation.

Golf skills will be tested on the the resort's two championship courses. The Ocean Course, designed by Robert Trent Jones, Sr. in 1947, boasts the famous island

ninth hole and 6,515 yards of links-like fairways rolling over gentle hills to well-maintained greens. The course plays to par 72.

Rumor has it that the Ocean's island hole was the inspiration for Pete Dye's No. 17 on the TPC's Stadium Course. Though the island includes a few bunkers and is a bit larger, the similarity between the two is unmistakable.

A product of architect Joe Lee, a Florida native, the 5,574-yard, par-70 Lagoon Course is a shotmaker's delight. The fairways are generous; however, numerous water hazards and small well-bunkered greens place a premium on accurate approach shots.

Though the Ponte Vedra Inn & Club pays homage to tradition, it has not blinded itself to today's

pampering resort lifestyle. In the Surf Club there are three pools, massage rooms, saunas and gourmet dining facilities. At the Seafoam Room, tri-level seating affords an enchanting view of the Atlantic Ocean.

Good news for those who bring their rackets as well as their clubs. The tennis complex has 15 all-weather, Har-Tru courts, seven of which are lighted. Other recreation alternatives at the 215-acre resort include swimming, surfing, sailing and jogging on one of the finest beaches you'll ever lay your soles on.

Most of the 202 rooms and suites have balconies or patios overlooking the Atlantic. In addition, there are golf cottages featuring fireplaces and balconies or patios.

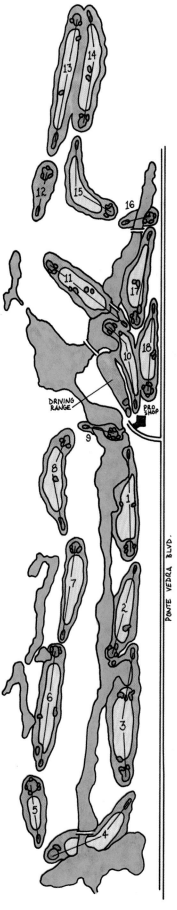

Address: 200 Ponte Vedra Blvd., Ponte Vedra Beach, Fla. 32082
Phone: (904) 285-1111, (800) 234-7842
No. of rooms: 202
No. of holes: 36
Sports facilities: tennis, spa, fitness center, sailing, volleyball and deep-sea fishing
Restaurants: 4
Business facilities: 20,000-square-foot conference center with 8 conference rooms and a grand ballroom
Location: Jacksonville area
Nearby attractions: Jacksonville Museum of Arts & Sciences, St. Augustine and Marineland

Ocean Course

Hole	Yards	Par
1	397	4
2	352	4
3	516	5
4	427	4
5	216	3
6	475	5
7	383	4
8	408	4
9	147	3
10	355	4
11	400	4
12	178	3
13	529	5
14	466	5
15	405	4
16	128	3
17	388	4
18	345	4
	6,515	**72**

Amelia Island Plantation
Amelia Island

With oaks and palmettos nearly enveloping the 1,250-acre resort, Amelia Island Plantation has the feel of a remote island. Located about 30 miles northeast of Jacksonville, Amelia Island Plantation is a symphony of massive sand dunes, large lagoons and sea oats.

Situated on the southern end of the island, the resort is nestled between the Intracoastal Waterway and the Atlantic Ocean. On the northern end of the 13½-mile island is Fernandina Beach, which has a 30-block national historic district of Victorian-era buildings.

Amelia Island Plantation has been one of Florida's most celebrated resorts since its opening in 1974. The resort offers 45 golf holes. The 27-hole Amelia Links layout, designed by Pete Dye, consists of the Oakmarsh (3,263 yards, par 36), Oysterbay (3,153 yards, par 35) and Oceanside (2,832 yards, par 35). Oakmarsh and Oysterbay feature twisting fairways, marsh edges and undulating greens. Sand dunes and sea oats border Oceanside.

The 6,750-yard, par-72 Long Point Course, designed by Tom Fazio, has dense forests of live oaks, red maples, cedars, pines and magnolias, dune ridges, and marsh and ocean views. This definitely is a good course for high handicappers because there are no cross-hazards — all hazards are parallel

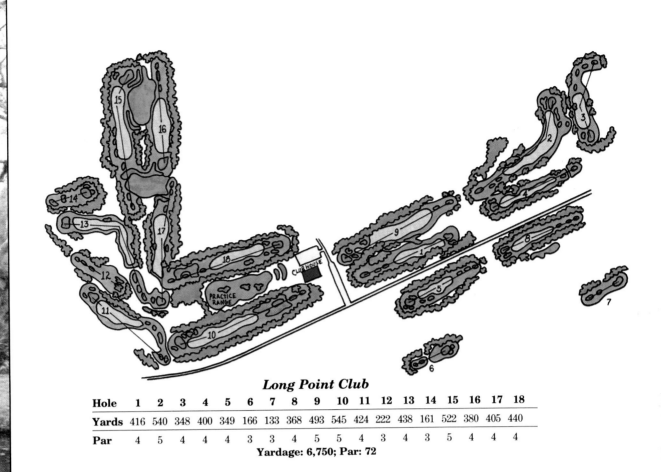

Long Point Club

Hole	1	2	3	4	5	6	7	8	9	10	11	12	13	14	15	16	17	18
Yards	416	540	348	400	349	166	133	368	493	545	424	222	438	161	522	380	405	440
Par	4	5	4	4	4	3	3	4	5	5	4	3	4	3	5	4	4	4

Yardage: 6,750; Par: 72

to the fairways.

Oceanfront holes Nos. 6 and 7, both par 3s, are among Florida's more picturesque. The 166-yard sixth hole plays from an elevated tee to a sharply undulating green. The seventh hole plays 133 yards through a narrow valley to a green surrounded by scraggy dunes. Club selection on both holes is dictated by the stiff right-to-left breezes.

There is a seemingly endless lineup of activities to be pursued at Amelia Island. There are 25 tennis courts, 4 miles of beach, a health and fitness center, and fishing in the numerous lagoons scattered throughout the property. Other pastimes include jogging or bicycling on a sunken forest trail and sport fishing charters for marlin, kingfish and tarpon.

Two types of accommodations are available — 256 hotel rooms and 296 one-, two-, three- or four-bedroom villas with complete kitchen facilities. High season is from mid-March to mid-May.

Address: State Road A1A, Amelia Island, Fla. 32034
Phone: (800) 874-6878
No. of rooms: 552
No. of holes: 45
Sports facilities: tennis, health and fitness center, horseback riding, fishing, biking and paddleboats
Restaurants: 5
Business facilities: 22,500-square-foot conference center and 6,000-square-foot Racquet Park Conference Center overlooking tennis courts
Location: Jacksonville area
Nearby attractions: Fernandina Beach historical district, Amelia Village shopping complex, Drummond Park

Ravines Golf & Country Club
Middleburg

In a state where most golf courses feature palm-dotted fairways as flat as your average landing strip, the Ravines is decidedly out of place. It's an extremely hilly course that looks like someone airdropped it in from the North Carolina highlands.

Nestled in heavily wooded terrain in the Jacksonville suburb of Middleburg, (40 minutes southwest of Jacksonville), the Ravines Golf and Country Club is a 10-year-old, 450-acre residential/resort community.

Designed by golf architect Ron Garl and PGA Tour pro Mark McCumber, a Jacksonville native, the 6,784-yard, par-72 course plays over, around and through deep, expansive ravines. Coming into play on seven holes, the ravines are 60 to 200 feet below the level of most of the terrain. One almost needs a four-wheel drive vehicle

rather than a golf cart to cover the course. Its hills are peppered with ancient hickories, live oaks and magnolias, rising up to 90 feet above sea level, and several of the holes play along the banks of Black Creek, which meanders along the layout.

How hilly is the Ravines? Well, on two holes you can't hit your blind approach until the group in front rings a big ship's bell to signal "all clear."

The Ravines' most unforgettable hole is No. 4, a 424-yard par 4. I suspect the reason golfers don't quickly forget the hole is that it gobbles up golf balls by the dozens. Even if you hit long and straight off the tee on the dogleg right layout, the second shot — over a large ravine to an island-in-a-jungle green — demands accuracy or it's drop time.

If you're really serious about

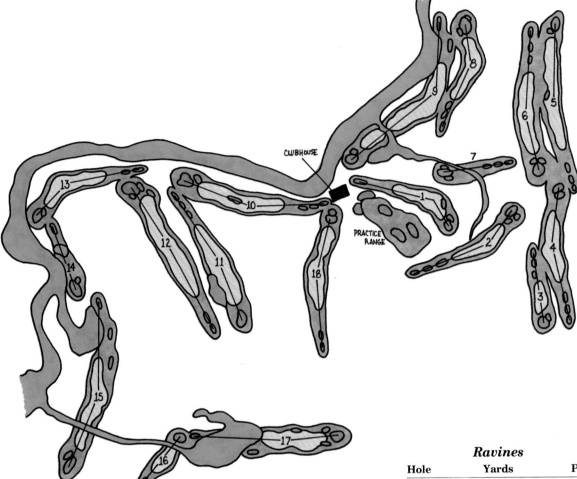

working on your putting, this is the place to do it. The Himalayas, an 18-hole consecutive putting facility, covering more than an acre, is similar to the large public putting green near the Old Course at St. Andrews, Scotland.

The Ravines has an unpretentious quality and can be likened to a rustic, albeit well-appointed backwoods retreat with amenities such as a clubhouse with restaurant, Olympic-size pool, tennis courts and boating facilities. There are 36 villas in the rental pool, which line the 18th fairway, and they feature such unusual amenities as beds that slide in and out of walls and room dividers.

Address: 2932 Ravines Road, Middleburg, Fla. 32068
Phone: (904) 282-1111
No. of rooms: 36
No. of holes: 18
Sports facilities: Olympic-size pool, tennis, fitness trail, fishing and boat dock
Restaurants: 2
Business facilities: 3 boardrooms
Location: Jacksonville area
Nearby attractions: Ravine State Ornamental Gardens, Jacksonville Landing Shopping Complex and St. Augustine

Ravines

Hole	Yards	Par
1	350	4
2	364	4
3	221	3
4	424	4
5	552	5
6	408	4
7	168	3
8	368	4
9	556	5
10	440	4
11	384	4
12	500	5
13	371	4
14	155	3
15	509	5
16	184	3
17	401	4
18	429	4
	6,784	**72**

Sheraton Palm Coast Resort
Palm Coast

Take 42,000 acres of former farm and timber land and add several golf courses, a resort hotel, 13,000 residents and countless recreational amenities and what you have is Palm Coast, one of the largest master-lanned communities in the United States.

Situated between St. Augustine and Daytona Beach, the 154-room Sheraton Palm Coast, perched beside the Intracoastal Waterway, is located in a "resort core" section of the community that puts an 80-slip marina, tennis club, pools and other activities within walking dis-

tance.

Each of the hotel's rooms, including two VIP suites, offers waterfront views of the Palm Coast Marina or waterway. Located next door is the Harbor Club vacation-ownership resort, where Sheraton guests enjoy free use of a pool, weight room, spa, miniature golf course and volleyball court. Complimentary transportation is provided to the golf course upon request. The courses are located minutes away from the hotel.

Leading the way is the 6,985-yard Matanzas Woods Course, a

par-72 design by Arnold Palmer and Ed Seay. It offers familiar Palmer trademarks like rolling fairways, large greens and different looks on each hole.

The Palm Harbor Course, designed by Bill Amick, is a 6,572-yard, par-72 test of skill with narrow fairways lined by huge oaks and palms, an abundance of water and 10 dogleg holes.

Palm Coast's longest course is the 7,074-yard, par-72 Pine Lakes, another Palmer-Seay design. It features tight fairways with rolling mounds along the sides and large,

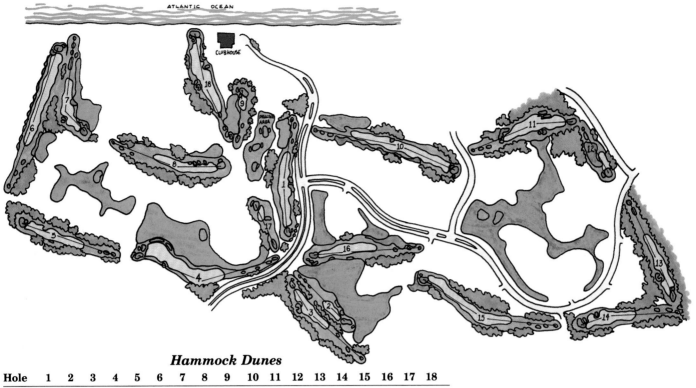

Hammock Dunes

Hole	1	2	3	4	5	6	7	8	9	10	11	12	13	14	15	16	17	18
Yards	434	245	360	547	370	534	366	404	181	525	373	198	366	386	524	396	200	393
Par	4	3	4	5	4	5	4	4	3	5	4	3	4	4	5	4	3	4

Yardage: 6,802; Par: 72

well-guarded greens.

Currently under construction, slated to open for play in December 1990, is the Cypress Knoll Course designed by Gary Player.

For a limited time, playing privileges also are available to hotel guests at Hammock Dunes, a private membership, oceanside community located on a barrier island across a bridge from the Palm Coast community.

Designed by Tom Fazio, the visually striking links-style Hammock Dunes course offers golfers three distinctive styles of play, from oceanfront greens to oak-lined fairways to grassy marshes. Measuring 6,802 yards and playing to par 72, Hammock Dunes already is considered one of the state's finest seaside courses.

Address: 300 Clubhouse Drive, Palm Coast, Fla. 32037
Phone: (904) 445-3000, (800) 325-3535
No. of rooms: 154
No. of holes: 72
Sports facilities: tennis, motor boat rental, fishing equipment rental, fitness center, biking and jogging paths
Restaurants: 1
Business facilities: 11,500 square feet of meeting space can accommodate up to 350 people
Location: St. Augustine area
Nearby attractions: St. Augustine, Daytona Beach and on-site shopping and dining

The Lodge at Ponte Vedra Beach
Ponte Vedra Beach

The Lodge at Ponte Vedra Beach, which opened in August 1989, already is being compared to the posh Lodge at Pebble Beach in California.

The $18 million lodge facility, located oceanside 21 miles south of Jacksonville, is a small, intimate hotel with an eye toward personal service. A Mediterranean-villa-style resort, it offers 66 luxuriously appointed guest rooms, including 24 suites, each with its own balcony overlooking Ponte Vedra Beach. Many rooms have whirlpool tubs and fireplaces.

If you're in the mood to be pampered, the Lodge was designed with you in mind. It offers services virtually unheard of at a resort of

Marsh Landing C.C.

Hole	Yards	Par
1	347	4
2	373	4
3	173	3
4	415	4
5	403	4
6	500	5
7	184	3
8	570	5
9	429	4
10	390	4
11	168	3
12	437	4
13	395	4
14	525	5
15	385	4
16	413	4
17	177	3
18	557	5
6,841		**72**

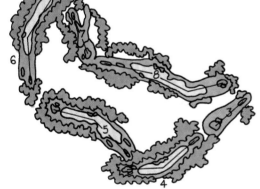

PRACTICE RANGE
CLUB HOUSE

its size. Among those: twice daily maid service, nightly turndown, 24-hour room service, a concierge and valet service.

The Mediterranean Room, with its oceanfront view, is a restaurant drenched in romantic ambience.

Lodge guests enjoy play-and-charge privileges at the Marsh Landing Country Club at Sawgrass, a five-minute drive from The Lodge. Transportation is provided upon request.

Designed by Ed Seay, the 6,841-yard, par-72 layout is named appropriately, as the marsh is utilized as a cross-hazard on several holes. It's unforgiving. Bring along an extra half dozen golf balls for this course.

One of my favorite holes, as well as one of the more picturesque is No. 7, a 184-yard par 3. It sports a large green framed by water, a rocky shoreline and several bunkers.

Golfers also may get tee times at either of two Tournament Players Club courses nearby.

If you start feeling a few aches and pains following a long day on the course, the impressive Bath Club offers a sauna, steam bath, whirlpool bath, massage rooms and three pools — two of which are oceanfront.

Address: 607 Ponte Vedra Blvd., Ponte Vedra Beach, Fla. 32082
Phone: (904) 273-9500, (800) 243-4304
No. of rooms: 66
No. of holes: 54
Sports facilities: pools, water sports equipment rental, deep-sea fishing and biking
Restaurants: 2
Business facilities: three facilities totaling 2,500 square feet of indoor, beachfront meeting space and 4,000 square feet of outdoor meeting space
Location: Jacksonville area
Nearby attractions: St. Augustine, Sawgrass Shopping Village, Jacksonville Landing shopping complex

Marriott at Sawgrass
Ponte Vedra Beach

Few resorts in the world offer as many great golf holes as the Marriott at Sawgrass. Along the Atlantic Ocean just south of Jacksonville, this resort has five golf courses, four driving ranges and seven putting greens. It's the only resort in the world that plays host to two TPC courses.

The headliner layout is the 6,857-yard, par-72 Tournament Players Club at the Sawgrass Sta-

dium Course. This Pete Dye masterpiece has been both praised and chastised since it opened in 1980. If you play only one Dye course in your life, this should be the one.

The Stadium Course gets its name from the built-in spectator bleachers that are unique to the course. The narrow fairways, lined with strips of sand, marsh grass and tall pines, strategically placed pot bunkers and fast greens, make

this course a marvelous test of your shotmaking skills. Want to know where your game stands? This is the course to find out. Caution: It's so difficult, you might not like the answer.

You can't talk about the Stadium Course without mentioning No. 17, the par-3 island hole, one of golf's most photographed holes. Accessible only by a narrow walkway, golfers must hit 132 yards over a lagoon into a stiff Atlantic breeze. If the course isn't crowded, you get two shots at the green; then it's drop time.

The 6,864-yard, par-72 TPC at Sawgrass Valley Course is the site of the Senior Tournament Players Championship. It, too, was designed by Dye, in collaboration with PGA pro Jerry Pate. Highlighting the masterfully crafted Scottishlike links is the 425-yard, par-4 finishing hole surrounded by large elevations on the left and water on the right.

Golfers encounter water on 24 of the 27 holes on the Sawgrass Country Club Course. The Florida State Golf Association ranks the 7,072-yard, par-72 East Rotation, designed by Ed Seay, as the toughest course in North Florida. On the 7,113-yard South rotation, golfers shoot a long par 5 over water twice to reach the water-encircled green.

Other courses include Marsh Landing, a 6,841-yard, par-72 layout; and Oak Bridge, which measures 6,345 yards and plays to par 70. Seay designed both.

Guests at the Marriott at Sawgrass have access to all the recreational amenities at Sawgrass, a 4,800-acre residential community. Among the choices: croquet, tennis, fishing and horseback riding.

Tournament Players Club
Stadium Course

Hole	Yards	Par
1	388	4
2	511	5
3	162	3
4	360	4
5	454	4
6	381	4
7	439	4
8	215	3
9	582	5
10	395	4
11	529	5
12	336	4
13	172	3
14	438	4
15	426	4
16	497	5
17	132	3
18	440	4
	6,857	**72**

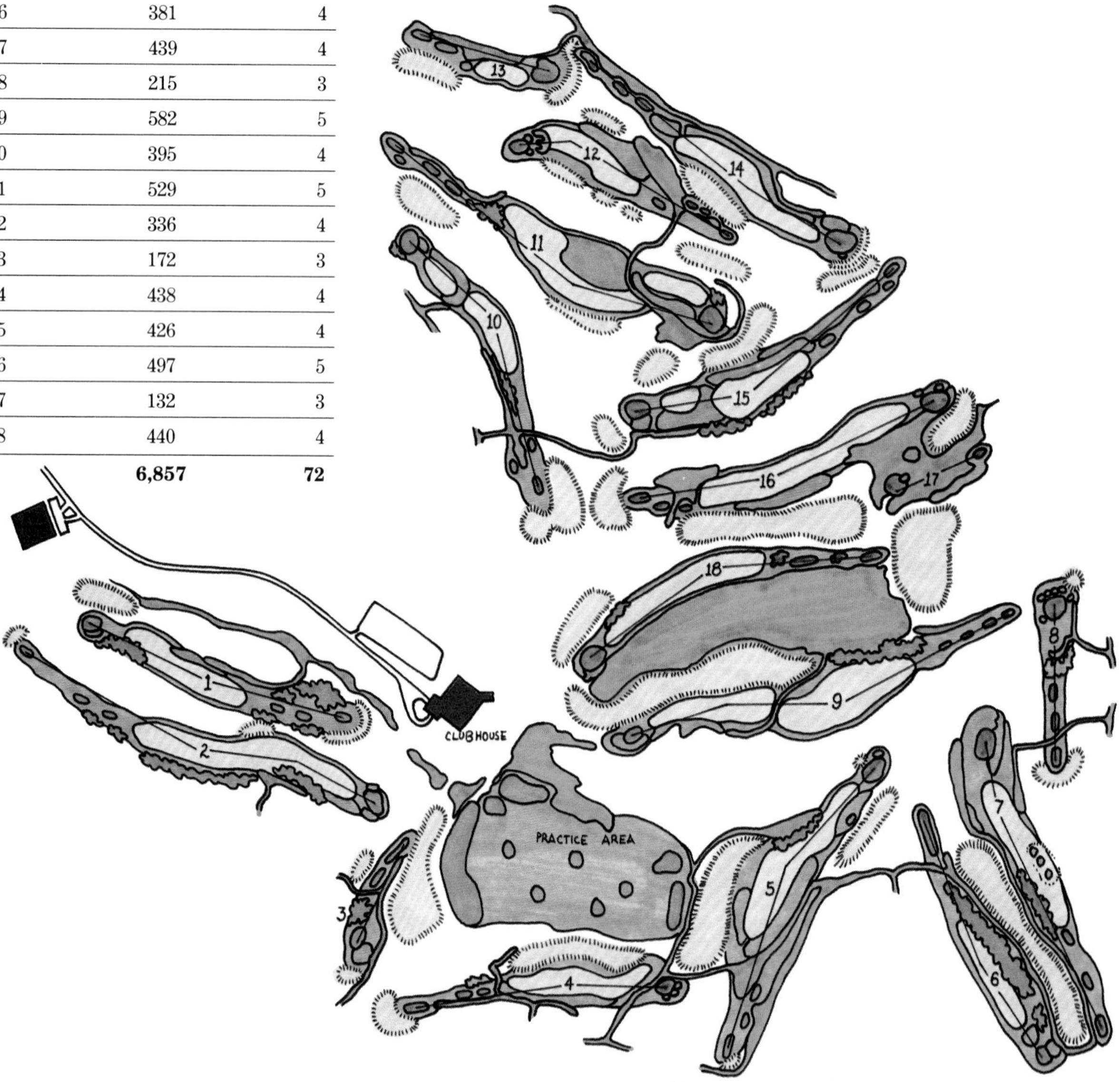

The Marriott at Sawgrass is popular with all sorts of golfers because of the variety of accommodations. There are a total of 557 guest rooms, suites, and golf and beachfront villas.

A favorite hangout after a day of golf is the Cascades, a lounge in the hotel's lobby that showcases a 70-foot atrium with skylight and a view of the Stadium Course's 13th hole. Here you can forget all about water balls, errant shots and sloppy swings.

Address: 1000 TPC Boulevard, Ponte Vedra Beach, Fla. 32082
Phone: (904) 285-7777, (800) 872-7248

No. of rooms: 557

No. of holes: 99

Sports facilities: tennis, croquet, horseback riding, fitness center and nature and biking trails

Restaurants: 3

Business facilities: 35,000 square feet of meeting and exhibit space, including five conference rooms and two executive boardrooms
Location: Jacksonville area
Nearby attractions: Sawgrass Village shopping complex, Jacksonville Landing, a riverfront marketplace with shops and restaurants, Marineland and St. Augustine

Best Of The Rest

The Summer Beach Resort & Country Club on Amelia Island, a 450-acre oceanfront resort and residential community, features a Mark McCumber course (6,805 yards, par 72) that has well-defined fairways and several greens of more than 10,000 square feet.

Another McCumber course that continually receives rave reviews from both duffers and low handicappers is Magnolia Point, a residential community in Green Cove Springs, southwest of Jacksonville. Its design is an eclectic one, with six holes that look and feel like the rolling hills of North Georgia, six like the pine woods of North Carolina and six, typical Florida level holes.

In Jacksonville, the 6,620-yard, par-71 Golf Club of Jacksonville, which opened in September 1989, is the PGA Tour's first venture into municipal golf. The course is short but challenging.

For those who want golf with a historical twist, the Donald Ross-designed 6,613-yard, par-71 course at the Ponce De Leon Resort in St. Augustine is reputed to be the state's oldest course and has been challenging golfers since 1916.

Summer Beach Resort & Country Club

Summer Beach Resort & Country Club (semiprivate)
5800 Island Parkway
Amelia Island, Fla. 32034
(904) 277-2525
18 holes

Magnolia Point (semiprivate)
3616 Magnolia Point Blvd.
Green Cove Springs, Fla. 32043
(904) 284-4653
18 holes

Golf Club of Jacksonville (public)
10440 Tournament Lane
Jacksonville, Fla. 32222
(904) 779-0800
18 holes

Ponce De Leon Resort
U.S. 1 North
St. Augustine, Fla. 32084
(904) 829-5314
18 holes

Other Courses To Consider

Fort George Island Golf Club (semiprivate)
11241 Ft. George Road
Fort George Island, Fla. 32226
(904) 251-3132
18 holes

Jacksonville Beach Golf Club (public)
605 South Penman Road
Jacksonville Beach, Fla. 32250
(904) 249-8600
18 holes

Jacksonville Naval Air Station Course (military I.D. required)
Composite Recreation Bldg. 620
Naval Air Station
Jacksonville, Fla. 32212
(904) 772-3249
18 holes

St. Augustine Shores Golf Course (semiprivate)
U.S. 1, South 295 Shores Blvd.
St. Augustine, Fla. 32084
(904) 794-0303
18 holes

5

Central Florida

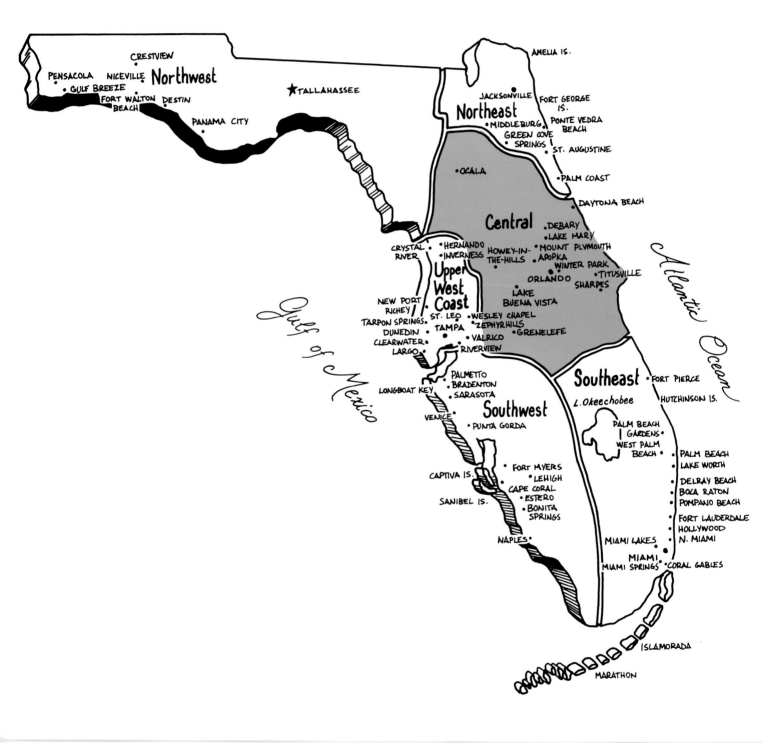

Overview

Engulfed by acres of sweet-smelling citrus groves and framed on the east by the Atlantic Ocean, Central Florida's engaging topography has produced some of the nation's greatest resort and residential community golf courses.

Designers like Jack Nicklaus, Robert Trent Jones, Sr., Arnold Palmer and Tom Fazio have crafted courses that reflect a myriad of styles. Whether it's Scottish, lakeside, flat, hilly, or artificially mounded, golfers have a dizzying number of divergent course designs from which to choose.

Better still for visiting golfers, few spots in the world provide the combination of first-class resort hotel accommodations and world-class golf that Central Florida offers. As one of the world's tourist meccas, thanks to Walt Disney World in Orlando, Central Florida has a tourism infrastructure that is second to none. Each year more than 12 million tourists visit the area.

Rising majestically from the flatlands is Orlando, a bustling metropolis with a parklike ambience enhanced by more than 50 lakes within the city limits.

The mention of Orlando to most non-Floridians usually will conjure up mental images of Mickey, Goofy and Shamu. Orlando, after all, is unquestionably the theme park capital of the universe. However, if you mention Orlando to any self-respecting golfer who has had the fortune of playing in the city, the images are likely to be decidedly different. Golf, without a doubt, is the most dominant feature of the city's sports scene.

There are more than 55 golf

Walt Disney World Resort

courses within a 30-mile radius of the city. Orlando is the only city in the country that plays host to two PGA Tour tournaments. The Nestle Invitational, formerly the Bay Hill Classic, is played in March. In October, golfers return to Orlando to participate in the Walt Disney Classic.

At last count, 22 PGA Tour members called Orlando home base (more than any other single area in the country) including Payne Stewart, Larry Rinker, Donnie Hammond and Nick Price, as well as part-time residents Arnold Palmer and Gary Player. As touring pro representative for the Grand Cypress Resort, Greg Norman, too, frequently can be seen tooling around town in his Maserati.

PGA Tour players of the future prep here — two minitours, the Florida Tour and the Spalding Space Coast Golf Tour, are played primarily on Orlando-area courses.

Orlando has been described as the "Harvard of golf instruction." It is home to several of the nation's most progressive golf instructional programs, including the Kinema-

Daytona Beach

tion Golf Studio at Heathrow, the Jack Nicklaus Golf Academy at Grand Cypress and the Walt Disney World Inn Golf Academy. In addition, highly acclaimed golf instructors John Redman, David Leadbetter, Phil Ritson and Fred Griffin teach in Orlando.

Golf is the sport of choice each January when Orlando plays host to the PGA Merchandise Show, the golf industry's largest trade show. Staged at the Orange County Convention and Civic Center, the show

Mission Inn Golf & Tennis Resort

Grand Cypress Resort

(not open to the public) attracts more than 600 companies each year.

Nearby communities north of Orlando such as Mount Dora, Apopka and Lake Mary have enjoyable courses that feature more trees and elevation changes than those in Orlando.

Ocala, 70 miles north of Orlando, a major breeding and training ground for thoroughbred horses, is noted for its verdant farmland and equally lush golf courses.

On the Atlantic Coast, Daytona Beach, home of the Ladies Professional Golf Association, has several notable layouts and a world famous 23-mile stretch of beach providing a wealth of off-the-course entertainment.

With an average annual temperature of 70 degrees, Central Florida is prime for golf year-round. Be aware, though, the sun is blistering in the summer. If you have a late morning or early afternoon tee time, by all means wear sun block and a hat or visor.

Central Florida has a subtropical climate, and between June and September most days see a shower, which lasts between 30 minutes and two hours. This region also is one of the country's most lightning-riddled areas. A corridor that

Grenelefe Resort and Conference Center

runs between Tampa and Orlando, dubbed "Lightning Alley," records more than 100 thunderstorm days a year.

If you have a family, your best scoring in Central Florida may well be away from the golf course. Central Florida has a wide spectrum of entertainment and recreation that is sure to make everyone happy. Theme-park hopping to world-renowned attractions like Walt Disney World, Epcot Center, Disney-MGM Studios, Universal Studios Florida, Sea World and Spaceport USA is enjoyed by children and adults of all ages.

During March, many golfers can play a round in the morning and then take in a spring training baseball game in the afternoon. The Boston Red Sox train in Winter Haven, the Houston Astros in Kissimmee, and the Kansas City Royals at Baseball City. Other spectator sports include jai alai, greyhound racing and auto racing. The Daytona 500, one of auto racing's premier events, is held each February in Daytona Beach.

For water sports enthusiasts, Daytona Beach, Cocoa Beach and other communities dotting the central Atlantic Coast offer everything from boating to deep-sea fishing.

Mission Inn Golf & Tennis Resort
Howey-in-the-Hills

At first glance, the Mission Inn Golf & Tennis Resort, with its quaint country inn nestled in the rolling hills north of Orlando, evokes images of Northern California, not Central Florida.

Spanish-Colonial in style, the inn rests on hilly terrain on the shores of Lake Harris and is reminiscent of the colorful and immaculately landscaped missions in Northern California. Just as those missions served as retreats more than a century ago, Mission Inn offers its version of an escape from the madding crowds and stress of everyday life.

Though many resorts tout their large size, Mission Inn emphasizes its quaintness and country environment. The Inn has 160 rooms, including 24 suites and 12 villas offering views of fairways, tennis courts and Lake Harris.

The courtyard is a popular spot to relax and soak up the atmosphere. You can lounge in the shade of the walls or stroll around while admiring the painted tile murals from Mexico and South America, the fountain and bell tower.

In a state known for predominantly flat golf courses, Mission Inn's layout is an anomaly. If you're in the mood to head for the hills, this is the Florida course for you. The elevation from tee to green can differ as much as 85 feet

on the par-72, 6,770-yard layout, which was designed and built by Scotsman C.C. Clarke 60 years ago and redesigned by Lloyd Clifton in 1970.

Perhaps the toughest hole at Mission Inn is No. 4, a 544-yard par 5 known as "Devil's Delight." From an elevated tee, the drive must carry over water to a narrow, tree-lined fairway. The second shot must adjust to a severe double dogleg. And the third shot has to carry over a wide bunker and a lake 50 to 75 yards wide into a sloping, well-trapped green.

Several of the par 3s feature island greens, and the eighth and 10th holes have a definite Scottish

Mission Inn

Hole	1	2	3	4	5	6	7	8	9	10	11	12	13	14	15	16	17	18
Yards	513	143	323	544	410	486	182	464	408	408	369	444	175	357	576	370	208	390
Par	5	3	4	5	4	5	3	4	4	4	4	4	3	4	5	4	3	4

Yardage: 6,770; Par: 72

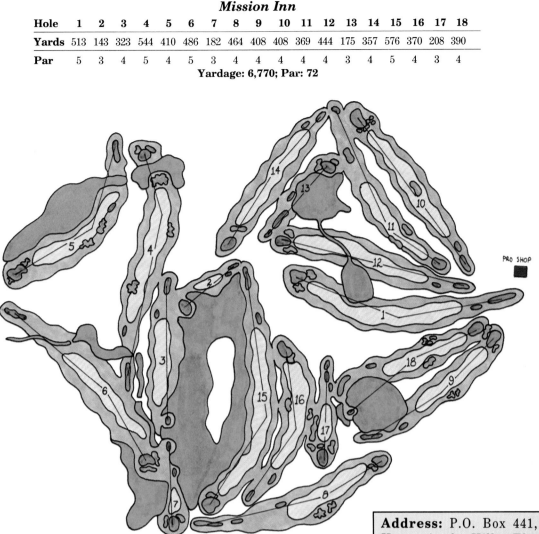

flavor.

Even if your score soars past the century mark, the placid surroundings will do much to soothe any frayed nerves. If it's instruction you need, Mission Inn has a golf school featuring video taping.

Golf is not all that Mission Inn has to offer. The resort's lineup of stress-busting recreational activities includes bass fishing in Lake Harris, cruises on a 1930s river yacht, tennis, volleyball, swimming and shuffleboard.

Address: P.O. Box 441, Howey-in-the-Hills, Fla. 32737

Phone: (800) 874-9053, in Florida (800) 342-4495, (904) 324-3101

No. of rooms: 160

No. of holes: 18

Sports facilities: tennis, marina, pool, bicycles, fitness room, volleyball and jogging course

Restaurants: 3

Business facilities: 11,000 square feet of meeting space, including a 5,000-square-foot conference center

Location: 30 miles northwest of Orlando on State Road 19

Nearby attractions: Walt Disney World, Epcot Center, Disney-MGM Studios, Universal Studios Florida and Sea World

Grenelefe Resort
Grenelefe

This resort is a golfaholic's dream come true. A different architect designed each of its three 18-hole championship courses to provide variety and challenge to golfers at every level.

Grenelefe's 7,325-yard, par-72 West Course, designed by Robert Trent Jones, Sr., is one of the state's longest courses. As with all Jones-designed courses, the layout is traditional, with long, tight fairways lined with pine trees and large, treacherous bunkers. The course consistently has been rated one of the best in Florida by numerous regional and national publications.

In contrast, the East Course, which plays to a par 72 and measures 6,802 yards, is much shorter and tighter than the rambling West Course. Designed by Ed Seay, the East Course is renowned for its first tee, positioned on the second story of Grenelefe's Conference Center, just outside the pro shop.

The South Course, designed by architect Ron Garl, with assistance

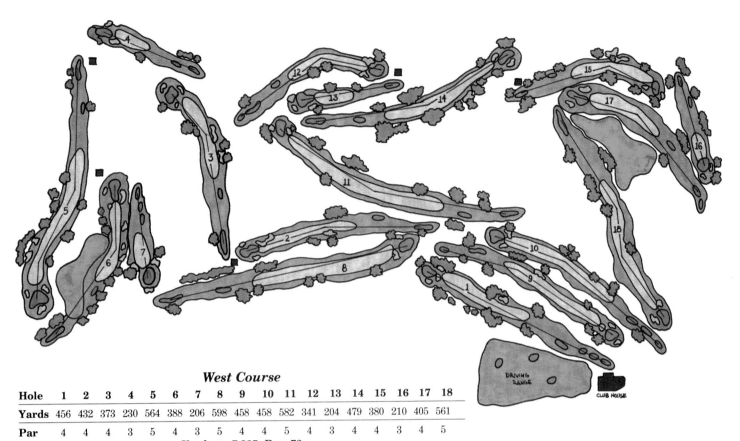

West Course

Hole	1	2	3	4	5	6	7	8	9	10	11	12	13	14	15	16	17	18
Yards	456	432	373	230	564	388	206	598	458	458	582	341	204	479	380	210	405	561
Par	4	4	4	3	5	4	3	5	4	4	5	4	3	4	4	3	4	5

Yardage: 7,325; Par: 72

from PGA touring pro Andy Bean, is a par-71, 6,869-yard masterpiece that, according to Garl, requires use of every club in the bag. Throughout the course, golfers will encounter hazards, including vast waste bunkers, wandering lagoons, large putting surfaces with steep tiers and island greens.

For those who want lower scores, Grenelefe is home to the Howie Barrow Golf School, which utilizes video analysis with a maximum of four students per instructor.

Grenelefe is a peaceful self-contained resort/residential community that stretches along the shores of 6,400-acre Lake Marion. Though Grenelefe was carved out of former citrus grove and ranch land, surprisingly it is a woodsy environment. The immaculately manicured, flower-laden common areas provide colorful accents to the al-ready beautiful oak-dotted landscape.

Despite being somewhat isolated, guests don't have to travel far for gourmet dining. The Green Heron, located on-site, is recognized as one of the best restaurants in Central Florida. Its menu features a variety of fresh fish, veal and chicken dishes and five-star service.

Grenelefe has 950 one- and two-bedroom villas in its rental program. These fairway villas include full living and dining rooms and kitchens with all the amenities of home. In addition, the resort has a small grocery store, post office, service station, florist shop, beauty shop and baby-sitting service.

The resort is 45 minutes from Orlando International Airport and 30 minutes from Walt Disney World, Sea World and Cypress Gardens.

Address: 3200 State Road 546, Grenelefe, Fla. 33844

Phone: (800) 237-9549, in Florida (800) 282-7875, (813) 422-7511

No. of rooms: 950

No. of holes: 54

Sports facilities: tennis, fishing, swimming and sailing

Restaurants: 4

Business facilities: 70,000 square feet of meeting space. including 32 meeting rooms and two large ballrooms

Location: Winter Haven area

Nearby attractions: Walt Disney World, Epcot Center, Disney-MGM Studios, Universal Studios Florida, Sea World and Cypress Gardens

Walt Disney World Resort
Lake Buena Vista

Even Mickey Mouse can play golf at the Walt Disney World Resort. Not only does the resort have 54 holes of championship golf, but it also features the Wee Links. The scaled-down championship course allows youngsters, adult novices and even theme park mascots to play golf at a serious, yet playable level.

Joe Lee designed the championship golf holes. The three courses serve as the site of the annual Walt Disney World/Oldsmobile Classic. However, you don't have to be a pro to be successful on these layouts, which are constructed to be especially forgiving to midhandicap players.

The wide-open 7,190-yard, par-72 Magnolia Course allows a mistake or two off the tee. In contrast, the Palm, a 6,957-yard, par-72 layout is shorter and tighter with more wooded fairways and water hazards. The Palm and Magnolia courses are located a 3-iron shot away from the borders of the Magic Kingdom. The Lake Buena Vista Course, noted for its narrow fairways, is a 6,655-yard, par-72 test of skill located near the Disney Village shopping complex.

The six-hole Wee Links, which soon will grow to nine holes, measures 1,529-yards with a par 22 and incorporates sand traps, water hazards, tees and greens just like an adult layout. The traps are small and flat, and the water hazards are shallow enough to allow easy ball retrieval. Holes on Wee Links are 5 inches in diameter compared with 4½ inches on a regulation course.

Magnolia Course

Hole	1	2	3	4	5	6	7	8	9	10	11	12	13	14	15	16	17	18
Yards	428	417	160	552	448	195	410	614	431	526	385	169	375	595	203	400	427	455
Par	4	4	3	5	4	3	4	5	4	5	4	3	4	5	3	4	4	4

Yardage: 7,190; Par: 72

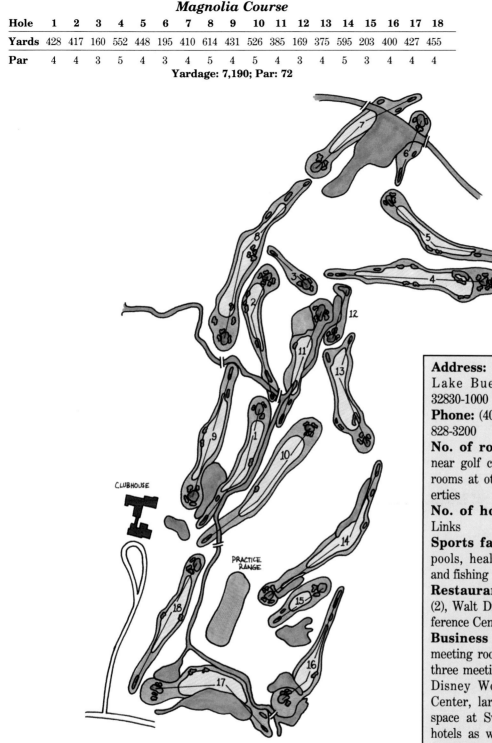

If you never have played golf or are just starting, this might be the place to capture a good swing before bad habits creep in. The Walt Disney World Golf Studio offers an instruction program with small classes. Instructors review each lesson on videotape and provide critiques. Students take home an audiocassette tape with suggestions and admonitions.

Guests can stay at the 288-room Disney Inn, which is surrounded by the Palm and Magnolia courses, the Walt Disney World Conference Center (near the Lake Buena Vista course) featuring 261 one-, two-, and three-bedroom condominium units and 324 minisuites, or any of the other many hotel properties in the park. Non-guests also are accorded playing privileges.

Address: P.O. Box 10,000, Lake Buena Vista, Fla. 32830-1000
Phone: (407) 824-2288, (407) 828-3200
No. of rooms: 873 on or near golf courses; additional rooms at other Disney properties
No. of holes: 54, 6 Wee Links
Sports facilities: tennis, pools, health club, boating and fishing
Restaurants: Disney Inn (2), Walt Disney World Conference Center (5)
Business facilities: One meeting room at Disney Inn, three meeting rooms at Walt Disney World Conference Center, large-scale meeting space at Swan and Dolphin hotels as well as other Disney properties
Location: On Walt Disney World property
Nearby attractions: Walt Disney World attractions, Pleasure Island nighttime entertainment complex, Walt Disney World Shopping Village, Universal Studios Florida and Sea World

65

Indigo Lakes Resort
Daytona Beach

Let's face it: When you think of Daytona Beach, images of spring break and auto racing generally come to mind. But golfers go there, too. Indigo Lakes Resort, on the corner of Interstate 95 and U.S. Highway 92, is home of one of the state's most highly rated golf courses.

Indigo Lakes is the new headquarters for the Ladies Professional Golf Association (LPGA). It also will play host to an LPGA tournament and will be used for the LPGA qualifying school.

A Lloyd Clifton product, the 7,123-yard Indigo course was cut out of a flat pine forest and is populated heavily with palms and palmettos. Bring your best putter because this layout has some of the largest greens in Florida, each averaging more than 9,000 square feet. The greens are so large there can be a three- or four-club difference from front to back depending upon the pin position.

Fairways on the course are large, too, but the 90-some sand traps and 50 acres of water scattered throughout the course will test just about every shot in your game.

If you're a slow starter and need a few holes to get your game going you might want to skip No. 2, a 535-yard par 5. Its narrow fairway is framed by a long lake on the right and a trap near the 250-yard mark on the left. If you hit right, club selection will not be difficult — just pull out the ball retriever.

Most physical and mental maladies acquired during a round of golf can be suitably addressed at the resort's fitness center and spa

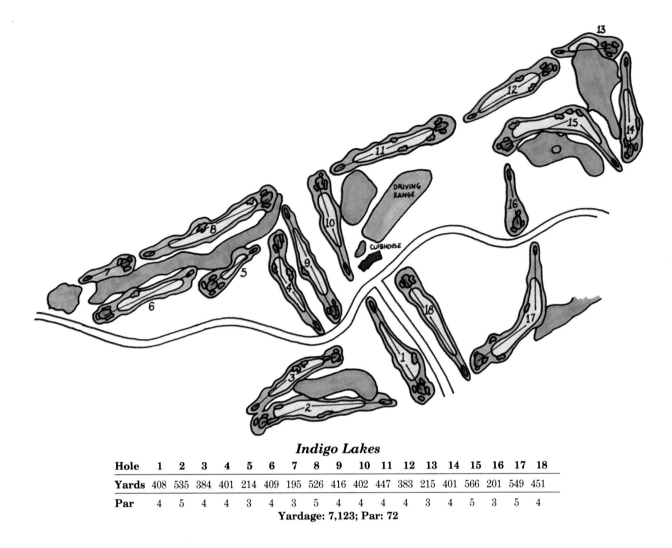

Indigo Lakes

Hole	1	2	3	4	5	6	7	8	9	10	11	12	13	14	15	16	17	18
Yards	408	535	384	401	214	409	195	526	416	402	447	383	215	401	566	201	549	451
Par	4	5	4	4	3	4	3	5	4	4	4	4	3	4	5	3	5	4

Yardage: 7,123; Par: 72

where whirlpools, saunas, steam rooms and a masseuse and masseur can soothe muscles and frustrations.

Other recreation besides golf includes tennis, swimming and racquetball.

The Indigo Inn has 212 rooms, including 64 executive suites, which offer either an executive king with king-size bed, study area, wet bar, bath and private patio or executive double with living/dining area, fully equipped kitchen, whirlpool bath, two double beds and a private patio.

Because of its location near ma-jor highways and the outskirts of Daytona Beach, there are numerous quality restaurants within a tee shot of the resort, including Major Moultries restaurant on-site.

Address: 2620 Volusia Ave., Daytona Beach, Fla. 32020

Phone: (800) 874-9918, in Florida (800) 223-4161, (904) 258-6333

No. of rooms: 212

No. of holes: 18

Sports facilities: tennis, racquetball and pools

Restaurants: 2

Business facilities: Conference Center can accommodate groups up to 400 people in 18 meeting rooms and banquet area

Location: Atlantic Coast Florida, 45 miles east of Orlando

Nearby attractions: Daytona International Speedway, St. Augustine, Kennedy Space Center, 23-mile-long Daytona Beach

Marriott's Orlando World Center
Lake Buena Vista

Picture the huge, opulent hotels that line the strip in Las Vegas and you'll have a fairly accurate image of this mega hotel situated on 200 acres in Lake Buena Vista, about 20 minutes from downtown Orlando.

Designed in a contemporary "Y" shape that gradually steps up to a 27-story tower, the hotel structure encircles a 5-acre activity court —

a picturesque setting of waterfalls, lagoons, pools, rockscapes and exotic landscaping.

A superbly designed 18-hole championship golf course wraps around the hotel on three sides. The 6,265-yard, par-71 layout, designed by Joe Lee, is open to guests at the resort complex as well as to the public. Lee has designed the course to require a vari-

Hole	Yards	Par
1	557	5
2	318	4
3	372	4
4	152	3
5	402	4
6	140	3
7	345	4
8	393	4
9	401	4
10	377	4
11	146	3
12	329	4
13	481	5
14	331	4
15	514	5
16	200	3
17	402	4
18	405	4
	6,265	**71**

ety of shots including low and run-up shots, fades, draws and an assortment of chip shots. Each tee is exceptionally long to allow for numerous tee marker placements that change the look and feel of the course.

Lee describes the course as a "thinking person's course, because the person who plans out each shot will definitely have the advantage."

One of the more visually appealing and challenging holes is the 200-yard, par-3 16th hole. The hole, surrounded by scrub oaks, is played from an elevated tee to a large green with plenty of opening on the right for the player who makes a mistake off the tee.

The perfect combination of woods, water (affecting 15 holes), palm trees, rockscapes, bridges and grass-sloped bunkers make this course a pleasurable 5-mile walk no matter how you play.

Because the course surrounds the hotel, views of the tees, greens and fairways are visible from almost every room. All of the hotel's 1,503 guest rooms feature cool tropical decor and spacious balconies. There are 101 suites, ranging from a one-bedroom Marriott Parlor to the International Suite, which features four adjoining bedrooms and an outdoor terrace.

Amenities abound with six restaurants, five lounges, 12 tennis courts, four pools, a health club and four hydrotherapy spas.

Address: 1 World Center Drive, Orlando, Fla. 32821
Phone: (407) 239-4200, (800) 228-9290
No. of rooms: 1,503
No. of holes: 18
Sports facilities: tennis, pools, health club
Restaurants: 6
Business facilities: 150,000 square feet of flexible meeting space
Location: Walt Disney World area
Nearby attractions: Walt Disney Magic Kingdom, Epcot Center, Disney-MGM Studios, Universal Studios Florida and Sea World

The Great Outdoors
Titusville

What do you get when you build a championship golf course on 2,000 acres of unspoiled wilderness and then stake out lots for recreational vehicles and surround those amenities with a $1 million clubhouse and tennis courts?

The answer is The Great Outdoors Premier RV/Golf Resort, which just might be the one spot to hook up to and never leave.

The Great Outdoors, the brainchild of Jack Eckerd, founder of the billion-dollar Eckerd Drugs empire, is set on a beautiful parcel of land with pristine lakes, sabal palms, oaks and pines off State Road 50 in east Central Florida, about five miles west of Titusville.

The innovative project offers RV sites for purchase much like a typical golf course community. Besides RV sites, there are park homes (small, modular-type homes with no more than 600 square feet of living space). For visitors, daily, weekly and monthly hookups are available from a rental pool of sites as well as park home rentals. Golf packages are offered, and the course also is open for public play.

The course is the crowning jewel of the amenity-rich Great Outdoors. This layout won't be confused with

the pitch-and-putt courses usually found at RV parks. Rather, the 6,705-yard, par-72 course is of a quality you might find at a high-priced golf community.

Hole	Yards	Par
1	569	5
2	408	4
3	442	4
4	170	3
5	357	4
6	365	4
7	351	4
8	172	3
9	521	5
10	356	4
11	164	3
12	419	4
13	450	4
14	540	5
15	321	4
16	175	3
17	405	4
18	520	5
	6,705	**72**

Playing the course, designed by Ron Garl, is much like walking through a wildlife preserve. Egrets and other birds always seem to be craning their necks to watch your shot. If you're lucky, you might even catch a glimpse of a deer or rabbit. There's a lot of water, and Garl left the palmetto, palm and pine terrain as natural as possible. The course is a good one for the average player because it has only 28 bunkers. When you consider the 442-yard, par-4 third hole has 10 bunkers, chances are that might be the only time in the round you'll need your sand wedge.

For competition types, you might want to crank up the RV in early December when The Great Outdoors plays host to the National RV Amateur Golf Championship, a 36-hole Callaway scoring tournament with trophies, prizes, gifts, parties and a cookout.

Like the first-class golf course, the rest of The Great Outdoors' amenities are ones you would not expect at an RV park. Amenities include a clubhouse and health club, heated pool, tennis courts, lighted shuffleboard, driving range and putting green. Another appealing element is the superb fishing on the property's 15 lakes, where largemouth bass, crappie and brim are the most popular catches. Golf course ponds 2, 5, 9, 11 and 14 have been stocked with bluegill and channel catfish.

Address: 4505 Cheney Highway (S.R. 50), Titusville, Fla. 32780
Phone: (800) 621-2267, (407) 269-5004
No. of rooms: 399 sites (all not in rental pool)
No. of holes: 18
Sports facilities: tennis, pool, shuffleboard, nature trails, canoeing and fishing
Restaurants: 1
Business facilities: 14,000-square-foot clubhouse
Location: Titusville area
Nearby attractions: Kennedy Space Center, Canaveral National Seashore, Sebastian Inlet State Park

Grand Cypress Resort
Lake Buena Vista

For those who always have dreamed of playing golf in Scotland but haven't gotten there, the next best thing just might be the Grand Cypress Resort, just off Interstate 4 near Lake Buena Vista.

It offers 45 holes of golf designed by Jack Nicklaus. Nicklaus has transported a slice of Scottish links land to Central Florida.

The 18-hole New Course, which resembles the Old Course at St. Andrews, Scotland, has similarities that include large and small bunkers, pot bunkers as deep as 12 feet, seven double greens and a snaking berm (creek). A stone bridge crosses a berm as it winds past the 18th hole, conjuring up images of the same hole at St. Andrews.

If you're not a good bunker player you might bring along a calculator to tally your score — strokes will add up quickly on this layout. The course has some 140 bunkers — the 9th hole alone has 21 bunkers — ranging from small pot bunkers to gaping bunkers, which have steps for access.

Very little water comes into play and few trees are located within the interior of the course, thus allowing ample room for drives.

The best time to play the New Course is in the winter, "when the fairways are hard, it's cold and the wind blows. It gives you the feel of Scotland," says Grand Cypress golf director Paul Celano. The New Course is 6,773 yards and plays to a par 72.

The North (3,521 yards), South (3,503 yards) and East (3,434 yards) nines all play to par 36. Highlighted by terraced fairways, moguls and platformed greens, the North and South nines, known as The Grand Cypress Course, play

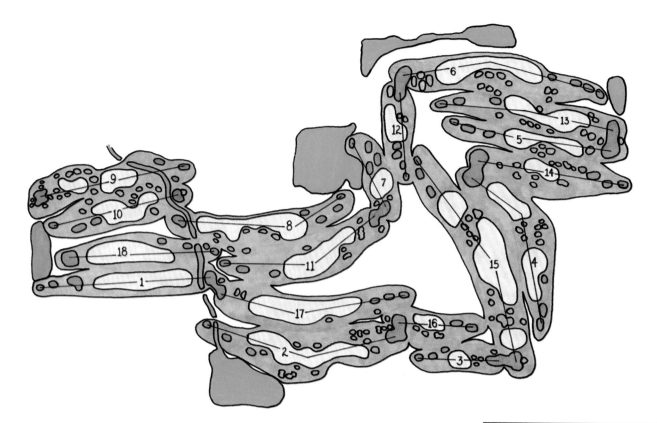

The New Course

Hole	1	2	3	4	5	6	7	8	9	10	11	12	13	14	15	16	17	18
Yards	362	514	179	440	393	496	182	440	382	330	430	207	431	371	570	190	485	371
Par	4	5	3	4	4	5	3	4	4	4	4	3	4	4	5	3	5	4

Yardage: 6,773; Par: 72

two to three shots more difficult than the New Course, Celano says.

Several big-name PGA Tour golfers practice at the Grand Cypress Resort. Among the more notable regulars are Greg Norman, Payne Stewart, Nick Price and Ian Baker-Finch.

The Grand Cypress Resort earned top honors when it was chosen by the International Golf Association as the site for the 1990 World Cup of Golf. It also was named a Gold Medal winner in *Golf Magazine's* "Best Golf Resorts in America."

The resort is home to the Jack Nicklaus Academy of Golf, one of the most innovative golf instruction facilities in the nation. Using the science of sports biomechanics with video, computer graphics and professional instruction, students receive a computer swing analysis and learn techniques to improve performance. The Academy includes its own three-hole teaching course, also designed by Nicklaus, which allows students to practice under a variety of playing conditions.

Resort guests stay at the towering 750-room Hyatt Regency. The hotel, which overlooks a 21-acre lake with 1,000 feet of white-sand beach, offers 72 suites and a half-acre, free-form pool with 12 waterfalls and three whirlpools. Golfers wanting accommodations on or near the golf courses can stay at the Villas of Grand Cypress. The one-, two-, three- and four-bedroom Mediterranean-style villas have full kitchens, dining rooms and verandas. Many units include fireplaces and whirlpool tubs.

Address: 60 Grand Cypress Blvd., Orlando, Fla. 32819

Phone: (800) 233-1234, (407) 239-1234

No. of rooms: 900

No. of holes: 45

Sports facilities: tennis, equestrian center, racquetball, sailing, canoeing, bicycling, jogging trail and croquet

Restaurants: 5

Business facilities: 57,000 square feet of meeting facilities, including a 25,000-square-foot ballroom and 27 meeting rooms. Also, 7,000-square-foot Executive Meeting Center near golf courses

Location: Walt Disney World area

Nearby attractions: Magic Kingdom, Epcot Center, Disney-MGM Studios, Universal Studios Florida, Sea World, numerous shopping areas

Best Of The Rest

Central Florida's best courses will either fulfill your dreams or create nightmares with their innovative designs. From replica holes to bigfoot bunkers to parking-lot size greens, the region's layouts have a plethora of the latest design features.

The Golden Ocala Golf Club on U.S. Highway 27 west of Interstate 75 in Ocala lets you get away to some of the world's finest golf holes without leaving Central Florida. Designed by Ron Garl, the 6,755-yard, par-72 layout has eight replica holes including the 129-yard, par-3 Postage Stamp at Royal Troon, and the 12th and 13th holes at Augusta National.

Orlando's most famous course is Bay Hill, the 7,086-yard, par-71 or par-74 Dick Wilson/Arnold Palmer masterpiece that is the site for the PGA's Nestle Invitational, formerly the Bay Hill Classic. Bay Hill is a private club. However, guests staying at the 64-room lodge are accorded playing privileges.

Ask an Orlandoan to name the best courses in the area and the layout at Timacuan, a golf course

Golden Ocala Golf Club

community in Lake Mary, 15 miles north of Orlando, is almost always mentioned. The 7,027-yard, par-72, Ron Garl-designed course plays like two different courses. The front nine is open with many high mounts, split-level fairways and large bunkers. By contrast, the back nine, heavily wooded with oak trees, native pines and sand hills, has a North Carolina flavor.

Golfers wanting hilly terrain should head for MetroWest, a 7,051-yard, par-72 course designed by Robert Trent Jones, Sr. The

MetroWest layout undulates with a variety of elevation changes. On several back-nine tees golfers can see the skyline of downtown Orlando, which is about 8 miles to the east.

Another popular hilly alternative is Errol Country Club, located in Apopka.

Lee Trevino fans should consider playing the La Cita Golf & Country Club where the "Merry Mex" has co-designed a 6,670-yard, par-72 course with Garl. La Cita is a private club, but guests staying at haciendas receive course privileges.

Golden Ocala Golf Club (semiprivate)
7300 U.S. 27 Northwest
Ocala, Fla. 32675
(904) 622-0172
18 holes

Bay Hill Club and Lodge (private-lodge privileges)
9000 Bay Hill Blvd.
Orlando, Fla. 32819-4899
(407) 876-2429
27 holes

Bay Hill

Timacuan Golf & Country Club

Timacuan Golf & Country Club
(semiprivate)
550 Timacuan Blvd.
Lake Mary, Fla. 32746
(407) 321-0010
18 holes

MetroWest Country Club
(semiprivate)
2100 Hiawassee Road
Orlando, Fla. 32811
(407) 297-0052
18 holes

Errol Country Club (private/
resort)
1355 Errol Parkway
Apopka, Fla. 32712
(407) 886-5000
27 holes

La Cita Golf & Country Club
(private/lodge privileges)
777 Country Club Drive
Titusville, Fla. 32780
(407) 267-2955
18 holes

Other Courses To Consider

Dubsdread Golf Course (public)
549 West Par Ave.
Orlando, Fla. 32804
(407) 849-2551
18 holes

Glen Abbey Golf Club
(semiprivate)
391 North Pine Meadow Drive
DeBary, Fla. 32713
(407) 668-4209
18 holes

Hunter's Creek Golf Course
(public)
14401 Sports Club Way
Orlando, Fla. 32821
(407) 240-4653
18 holes

International Golf Club (public)
6351 International Golf Club Road
Orlando, Fla. 32821
(407) 239-6909
18 holes

Mount Plymouth Golf Club
(semiprivate)
249 Pine Valley Drive
Mount Plymouth, Fla. 32776
(904) 383-4821
18 holes

Patrick Air Force Base Golf
Course (military)
Patrick Air Force Base, Fla. 32925
(407) 494-7856
18 holes

Sam Snead Executive Golf Course
(public)
4255 North U.S. Highway 1
Sharpes, Fla. 32959
(407) 632-2890
18 holes

Winter Pines Golf Club
(semiprivate)
950 South Ranger Road
Winter Park, Fla. 32792
(407) 671-3172
18 holes

Ventura Country Club
(semiprivate)
3201 Woodgate Blvd.
Orlando, Fla. 32822
(407) 277-2640
18 holes

6

Upper West Coast Florida

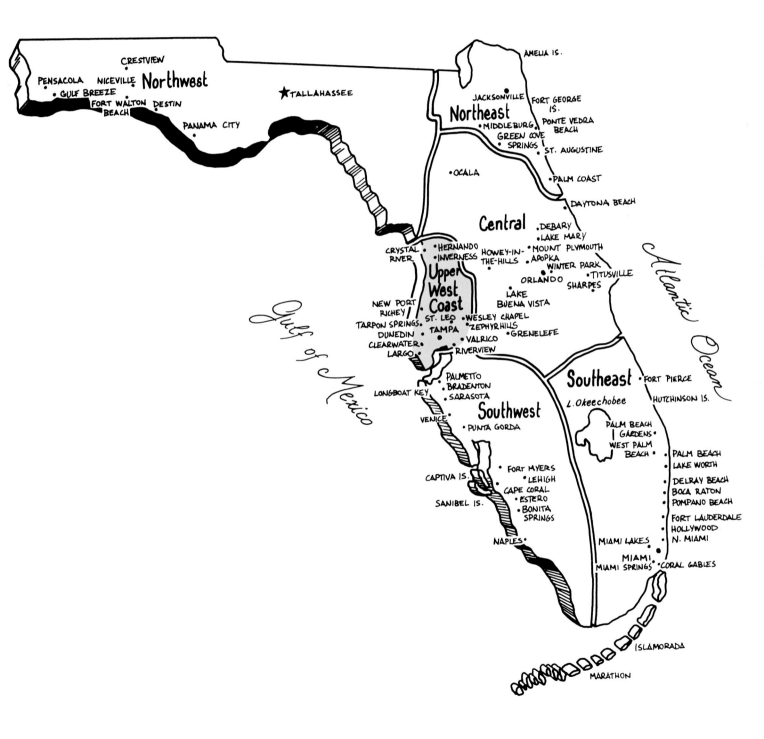

Overview

If you want to sample the full breadth of Florida culture in addition to playing a variety of golf courses, this region can accommodate both.

In the northern reaches, visitors can immerse themselves in an "Old Florida" lifestyle where much of the pine-dotted rolling terrain hasn't been scarred by development. Here, the pace is unhurried. It's a place where folks still wave at strangers as they race by on Highway 19, the region's main thoroughfare.

Towns like Cedar Key, Crystal River and Inverness, quaint and rustic settings, are the antithesis of Florida's more heralded and more touristy locales farther down the peninsula. Admittedly, there are fewer golf courses in this part of the state, yet generally they're less crowded and you won't have to endure the golf cart traffic jams so prevalent in many South Florida areas during the height of the tourist season.

The uniquely wooded terrain has been the ideal palette for designers to create layouts with personalities that favor North Carolina or Georgia more than Florida. Make no mistake, this is pine, not palm country.

On the other end of the culture spectrum is the palm-laden Tampa Bay area, which is one of Florida's most dynamic cities. With its shimmering buildings stretching skyward along the bay, Tampa serves notice it's one of Florida's fastest growing cities. Tampa is a unique, exciting urban center brimming with cultural activities, shopping, historical sights and best of all, golf courses.

Innisbrook Resort

The Tampa area has more than 40 golf courses. With a significant number of executive layouts the city has a wealth of opportunities for novices or golfers who want to work on their iron play.

Some of Tampa's most challenging courses are within residential communities where top architects were recruited to design layouts that would turn heads and sell homes. As a result, the courses, several of them semiprivate that allow the public to play, have many unique design features that would give any pro or low-handicapper a challenge.

Across the bay in Clearwater, the lifestyle is sun and fun. The courses are covered predictably with a lot of sand and palm trees. So if you want the tropical look, you've come to the right place.

For the most part, the Upper West Coast of Florida, according to tourism officials, draws the largest percentage of its visitors and new residents from the upper Midwest — such as Illinois, Michigan, Ohio and Indiana.

Tampa

Saddlebrook Resort

The weather in the Upper West Coast sometimes differs greatly from north to south. Some winter days in the northern areas are so bone-chilling you'll need a hefty wool sweater or jacket.

Though Tampa has a few chilly days each winter, generally the weather is agreeable and courses are playable year-round. You're more likely to find 75- to 80-degree temperatures in late November, December and January.

During the fall, Tampa just might be the best place on earth to play golf. Tampa's weather during the fall is the closest thing to perfect with a warm sun and a faint, steady breeze from the bay providing the perfect conditions.

If you're a sports fan, you'll be busy off the course as well. The Upper West Coast plays host to professional sports, including the NFL's Tampa Bay Buccaneers and major-league baseball teams such as the Toronto Blue Jays (Dunedin), Cincinnati Reds (Plant City) and Philadelphia Phillies (Clearwater), which hold their spring training in the region.

Tampa Bay Downs is the site for thoroughbred horse racing, and the greyhounds run in Tampa.

With the turquoise waters of the Gulf of Mexico never more than a 30-minute drive away, this region has plenty to offer, whether visitors want a quiet, isolated beach or a night out on the town.

Saddlebrook Resort
Wesley Chapel

County Road 54, which leads to Saddlebrook, is framed on each side by uninspiring flat ranch land. However, once inside the gates of Saddlebrook, your senses are overwhelmed by the natural beauty of the wooded countryside and flower-laden landscape. It's almost as if you've driven into a dream that you don't want to end. The winding road weaves through countryside dotted with tall cypress, pines, palms and lakes.

Featuring two 18-hole Arnold Palmer courses (with design assistance from Dean Refram), this 480-acre resort 20 miles northeast of Tampa is recognized by many golfers as the quintessential Florida golf resort. It combines superbly designed golf holes with plentiful amenities.

The courses are not long, but they are challenging, nonetheless, because of the difficulty of the rolling terrain. The fairways dip and roll like a roller coaster. Tall cypress and pine trees line the fairways. The greens, with their many undulations, resemble Palmer's Bay Hill course in Orlando. Both Saddlebrook courses play to par 71; the Saddlebrook Course measures 6,642 yards, and the Palmer Course is 6,469 yards.

Typical of Palmer's design wizardry is the par-4, 390-yard first hole on the Saddlebrook course, which is narrowed in the target area by water and marsh. Water runs the length of the right side, and a gentle dogleg begins 200 yards out. It's not exactly a confidence-builder, but it's a hole you'll want to play again and again.

For golfers and other sports enthusiasts who want to maximize performance, Saddlebrook offers innovative programs in its sports and health development department. Headed by Dr. Jack Groppel, a leading authority and pioneer in the field of sport biomechanics, the program is designed to

Palmer Course

Hole	1	2	3	4	5	6	7	8	9	10	11	12	13	14	15	16	17	18
Yards	423	191	445	560	383	355	156	495	360	368	510	391	161	411	397	347	373	143
Par	4	3	4	5	4	4	3	5	4	4	5	4	3	4	4	4	4	3

Yardage: 6,469; Par: 71

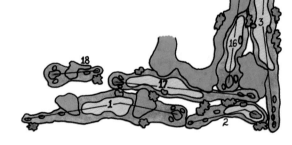

maximize physical and mental potential through the sport sciences. Topics addressed include stress management, time management and nutrition.

One of the pleasurable features of Saddlebrook is its unique walking village concept with condominiums clustered around centralized amenities. The focal point of the walking village is the 270-foot-long pool. Also within walking distance are the golf clubhouse, tennis facilities, health club/spa and restaurants.

Guests stay in California-contemporary-styled condominiums that feature hotel-type rooms or one-, two- and three-bedroom suites. Many of the accommodations have patios or balconies that overlook the golf course or a pond.

Address: 100 Saddlebrook Way, Wesley Chapel, Fla. 33543
Phone: (813) 973-1111, (800) 237-7519, in Florida (800) 729-8383
No. of rooms: 500
No. of holes: 36
Sports facilities: tennis, health spa and fitness center, deep-sea fishing and pool
Restaurants: 4
Business facilities: 60,000 square feet of meeting and function space, including Pegasus Ballroom, which can be divided into 10 sections
Location: 20 miles northeast of Tampa, 1 mile east of Interstate 75
Nearby attractions: Busch Gardens, Walt Disney World, Epcot Center, Disney-MGM Studios, Universal Studios Florida, Sea World

Plantation Inn & Golf Resort
Crystal River

If you're looking for a laid-back resort experience where golf clothes are the fashion statement on and off the course, this resort may be your kind of place. Plantation Inn & Golf Resort, on the shores of the Crystal River 70 miles north of Tampa on U.S. Highway 19, has a gracious "kick-off-your-shoes" ambience.

The Plantation, with 27 holes of championship golf, is the home of the Florida Women's Open, held each fall. Designed by Mark Mahannah in 1958, the beautifully manicured course combines dozens of natural lakes, carefully placed sand traps and loblolly pines.

The variety of tee placements makes Plantation an ideal spot for husbands and wives to enjoy playing a round of golf together. The

original 18-hole course measures 6,644 yards and plays to a par 72. The Lagoon nine-hole course is a par-33, 2,511-yard layout.

The Plantation features The Golf School, which has one of the

Championship Course

Hole	Yards	Par
1	340	4
2	345	4
3	197	3
4	485	5
5	430	4
6	330	4
7	540	5
8	182	3
9	351	4
10	429	4
11	560	5
12	426	4
13	430	4
14	365	4
15	195	3
16	494	5
17	185	3
18	370	4
	6,644	**72**

Lagoons Nine

Hole	Yards	Par
1	255	4
2	185	3
3	315	4
4	360	4
5	341	4
6	340	4
7	415	4
8	155	3
9	145	3
	2,511	**33**

longest traditions of any school in the country.

Golfers who also enjoy fishing should bring their rods and reels along with their clubs. The Crystal River is one of the state's best fishing areas, with trout, redfish and bass the top catches. A favorite activity is to fish all morning, accompanied by a guide, and eat your catch for lunch on a nearby island.

Fed by 13 freshwater springs, the Crystal River near the Plantation is a favorite snorkeling and diving location. A full-service marina behind the resort offers rental boats, snorkeling and scuba equip-

ment, experienced guides, and complete docking and boat launching facilities.

For recreation on *terra firma,* there are four lighted tennis courts.

The Plantation's white, columned inn conjures up images of traditional Southern hospitality — and that's just what you get at this folksy resort. You won't see many blazers with insignias. The emphasis at the Plantation is on relaxation the old-fashioned way. Accommodations include 124 deluxe rooms, seven one-room suites, 12 golf villas and six three-bedroom condominiums.

Address: P.O. Box 1116, Crystal River, Fla. 32629

Phone: (904) 795-4211, eastern U.S. (800) 632-6262

No. of rooms: 149

No. of holes: 27

Sports facilities: on-site marina, fishing, tennis and scuba diving

Restaurants: 2

Business facilities: 7,700-square-foot conference center

Location: 70 miles north of Tampa

Nearby attractions: Crystal River, 6 miles from Gulf of Mexico, Homosassa Springs

Belleview Biltmore Resort Hotel
Clearwater

Often referred to as "The Grand Dame" of Florida's west coast, the Belleview Biltmore is a monument to an era of elegance and grace. It is Florida's answer to the huge, luxurious hotels in European capitals like Paris and Vienna. Built in 1897 by railroad tycoon Henry B. Plant, the hotel was one of the nation's first to feature golf as an amenity. Many believe it was the hotel that began the movement of golf from the confines of the country club to the resort hotel.

The large rambling Victorian-style hotel, with its white walls, green gables and sweeping verandas, rests in a postcard setting of carpetlike lawns, palms, water oaks and native pines overlooking the Gulf of Mexico.

Listed on the National Registry

of Historic Places, the often-renovated and up-to-date Belleview Biltmore reputedly is the largest occupied wooden structure in the world.

The resort offers guests playing privileges on three courses. De-

signed by the dean of American golf architects, Donald J. Ross, the three layouts are unique in coastal Florida and represent Ross at the peak of his creative powers.

The East (6,391 yards, par 71) and West (6,367 yards, par 71) courses at the Bellair Country Club, just steps away from the hotel's front lobby, are two of Florida's oldest courses, though both were renovated in 1973. Spreading over a long, high bluff — the highest elevation in all coastal Florida — the fairways follow the natural terrain and features of the land as Ross found them. Creeks and ravines cut through the high plateau and there are many natural water hazards.

The Pelican Country Club tract measures 6,485 yards and plays to

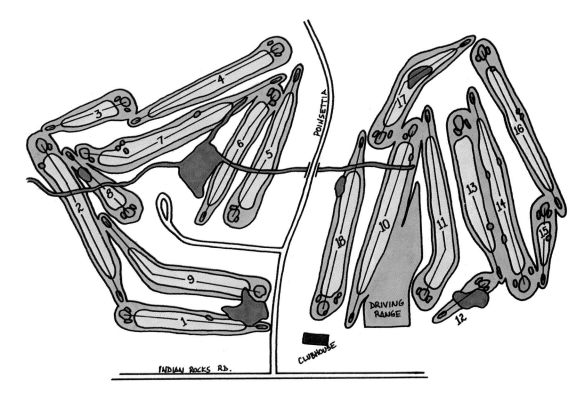

Pelican Country Club

Hole	1	2	3	4	5	6	7	8	9	10	11	12	13	14	15	16	17	18
Yards	346	407	192	375	401	325	500	192	485	449	472	140	374	476	178	381	383	409
Par	4	4	3	4	4	4	5	3	5	4	5	3	4	5	3	4	4	4

Yardage: 6,485; Par: 72

par 72.

Those who want to fine tune their swing will find the Florida Golf School at the Belleview Biltmore a helpful program. A typical day includes five hours of lessons, utilizing a specially designed practice area as well as the resort's three courses.

The Belleview Biltmore's ambience undoubtedly is one of an opulent era long ago, but make no mistake, the amenities definitely are up-to-date. Most impressive is a European-style spa added in 1985. No matter what the order, whether you want to be exercised, toned, massaged or refreshed, this full-service facility can fill the bill.

The rooms and suites exude old-world European flavor. There are 310 guest rooms, 40 suites and a variety of connecting rooms ideal for families.

The Queen Anne decor is consistent with the Victorian style of the exterior. In the suites, French doors trimmed in white wood separate the sleeping area from the seating area.

Perhaps the most striking interior beside the lobby is the Tiffany Dining Room, named for its priceless vaulted stained glass ceiling. It's a one-of-a-kind dining experience.

Address: 25 Belleview Boulevard, Bellair/Clearwater, Fla. 34616
Phone: (813) 442-6171, (800) 237-8947, in Florida (800) 282-8072
No. of rooms: 350
No. of holes: 54
Sports facilities: tennis, pools, health club and spa, volleyball, croquet, bicycle and sailboat rentals
Restaurants: 4
Business facilities: 30,000 square feet of function space, 14 individual meeting rooms
Location: Clearwater area
Nearby attractions: SeaEscape one-day cruises, Salvador Dali Museum, Sunken Gardens

Innisbrook
Tarpon Springs

Innisbrook is one of Florida's more celebrated golf resorts and deservedly so. It combines 63 holes of world-class golf with so many amenities that one hardly can count them all, much less utilize all of them during a single visit.

The 1,000-acre resort is located 25 minutes from Tampa International Airport just south of Tarpon Springs, a Greek fishing village.

Low-handicappers, start your golf carts! The Copperhead course, Innisbrook's flagship layout, is a par-71 course with 27 holes and measures 6,836 to 7,031 yards — depending on which combination of nines is played.

Copperhead No. 1 is the longest of the three nines at 3,588 yards. Copperhead No. 2 is 3,443 yards and Copperhead No. 3 measures 3,393 yards. How testy is Copperhead? Well, there are only three straightaway holes on No. 1, and two of those are par-3 holes.

Copperhead has few lateral water hazards and the rolling hills and tall pines are reminiscent of the Sandhills of North Carolina. If

you can go 18 holes without hitting at least one branch on this tree-laden layout, then it might be time

to check the dates for the PGA Tour qualifying school. One of the course's newest features is the annual flower bed arrangements at every tee, with spectacular designs on Copperhead No. 1's fifth hole and Copperhead No. 3's sixth hole.

Innisbrook's two other 18-hole championship layouts include the 6,999-yard, par-72 Island Course and the 6,006-yard Sandpiper Course, which plays to par 70. E. Lawrence Packard designed all 63 holes.

For the Island and Sandpiper courses the appropriate dress might be scuba gear if you're not a straight hitter. The Island's first six holes are dominated by lateral water hazards that require accuracy on tee shots and approaches. On the Sandpiper, water hazards must be negotiated on 11 holes, sometimes on both sides of the fairway.

Regardless of which course you select, the golf holes at Innisbrook

Innisbrook Course 1

Hole	1	2	3	4	5	6	7	8	9
Yards	540	403	436	165	539	459	385	235	426
Par	5	4	4	3	5	4	4	3	4

Yardage: 3,588; Par: 36

Innisbrook Course 2

Hole	1	2	3	4	5	6	7	8	9
Yards	451	552	382	175	571	212	465	211	424
Par	4	5	4	3	5	3	4	3	4

Yardage: 3,443; Par: 35

Innisbrook Course 3

Hole	1	2	3	4	5	6	7	8	9
Yards	375	516	145	307	414	544	430	198	464
Par	4	5	3	4	4	5	4	3	4

Yardage: 3,393; Par: 36

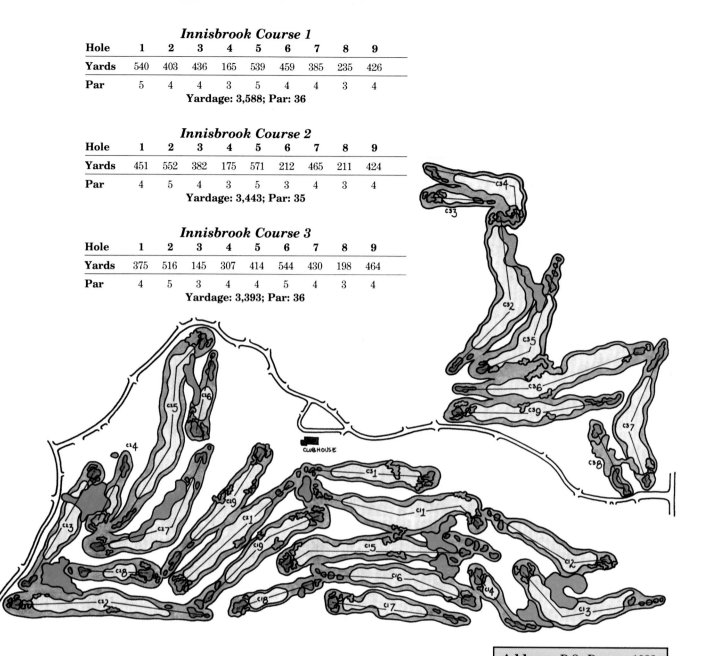

are impeccably maintained and beautiful. Each of the three has its own clubhouse complex, complete with restaurants (from gourmet to standard American) and pro shop.

If this sounds a bit too much for your level of play, you might want to enroll at the Innisbrook Golf Institute. Developed by director of golf and former All-America golf professional Jay Overton, the Golf Institute is a year-round series of intensive instructional clinics using the latest in audio-visual teaching aids with a 4-to-1 student to professional ratio.

Low-handicappers and beginners will find the Institute challenging and educational.

A partial list of activities and amenities at Innisbrook includes: 18 tennis courts, four indoor racquetball courts, six pools, a health club, jogging trails, bicycle rentals, nature walks, tanning facilities and a beauty salon.

The 1,000 guest suites are contained in 28 low-rise lodges. Because the lodges are spaced generously throughout the property, you never get the sense of a crowded resort even though all the suites might be occupied. Among the four types of accommodations available are the club suite, which offers a large parlor and a twin-bedded bedroom and the 2,000-square-foot, two-bedroom deluxe suite.

Address: P.O. Drawer 1088, Tarpon Springs, Fla. 34688
Phone: (800) 456-2000
No. of rooms: 1,000
No. of holes: 63
Sports facilities: tennis, fitness center, 6 pools, nature and jogging trails
Restaurants: 4
Business facilities: 3 conference buildings comprising 65,000 square feet of meeting space, 39 seminar rooms
Location: 20 miles north of Tampa
Nearby attractions: Tarpon Springs Greek fishing village, Busch Gardens, fishing

Best Of The Rest

Bloomingdale Golfers Club

How about a walk on the wild side? The Bloomingdale Golfers Club, located in Valrico just east of Tampa, embodies the natural look with an abundance of wildlife. The golf course's residents include a bald eagle and about 60 species of semi-rare birds. Designed by Ron Garl, the 7,155-yard, par-72 layout is a wonderland of tree-lined fairways, massive waste areas, deep grass bunkers and 13 lakes.

For a course that looks and plays like the wind-swept links of Scotland, the Summerfield Golf Club, situated 20 minutes east of downtown Tampa, is the closest thing to being there. Unobstructed breezes from nearby Tampa Bay complement the experience along with mounds, no-mow roughs and sandy waste areas. The 6,944-yard, par-71 Summerfield layout also was designed by Garl.

In Largo, near Clearwater, the venerable Bardmoor Country Club, formerly the site of the JC Penney Classic, has three excellent courses (two of which are open to the public).

Bloomingdale Golfers Club (semiprivate)
1802 Nature's Way Blvd.
Valrico, Fla. 33594
(813) 685-4105
18 holes

Summerfield Golf Club (semiprivate)
13050 Summerfield Blvd.
Riverview, Fla. 33569
(813) 671-3311
18 holes

Bardmoor Country Club (semiprivate)
8000 Bardmoor Blvd.
Largo, Fla. 34647
(813) 397-0483
54 holes

Dunedin Country Club (semiprivate)
1050 Palm Blvd.
Dunedin, Fla. 34698
(813) 733-7836
18 holes

Links of Lake Bernadette (semiprivate)
111 Links Land Road
Zephyrhills, Fla. 34248

Other Courses To Consider

Airco Golf Club (public)
3650 Roosevelt Blvd.
Clearwater, Fla. 34622
(813) 573-4653
18 holes

Babe Zaharias Golf Club (public)
11412 Forest Hills Drive
Tampa, Fla. 33612
(813) 932-8932
18 holes

Bayou Golf Club (semiprivate)
1000 Belcher Road
Largo, Fla. 34647
(813) 546-3099
9 holes

Citrus Hills Golf & Country Club (semiprivate)
500 East Hartford St.
Hernando, Fla. 32642
(904) 746-4425
36 holes

East Bay Country Club (semiprivate)
702 Country Club Drive
Largo, Fla. 34641
(813) 581-3333
18 holes

Hunter's Green Country Club (semiprivate)
18101 Longwater Run Drive
Tampa, Fla. 33647
(813) 973-1000
18 holes

Inverness Golf & Country Club (semiprivate)
3150 South Country Club Drive
Inverness, Fla. 32650
(904) 637-2526
18 holes

MacDill Air Force Base Golf Club (military)
P.O. Box 6001
Tampa, Fla. 33608
(813) 830-2200
36 holes

Magnolia Valley Golf & Country Club (semiprivate)
7223 Massachusetts Ave.
New Port Richey, Fla. 34653
(813) 847-2342
27 holes

St. Leo Abbey Golf Club (semiprivate)
S.R. 52 West
St. Leo, Fla. 33574
(904) 588-2016
18 holes

7

Southwest Florida

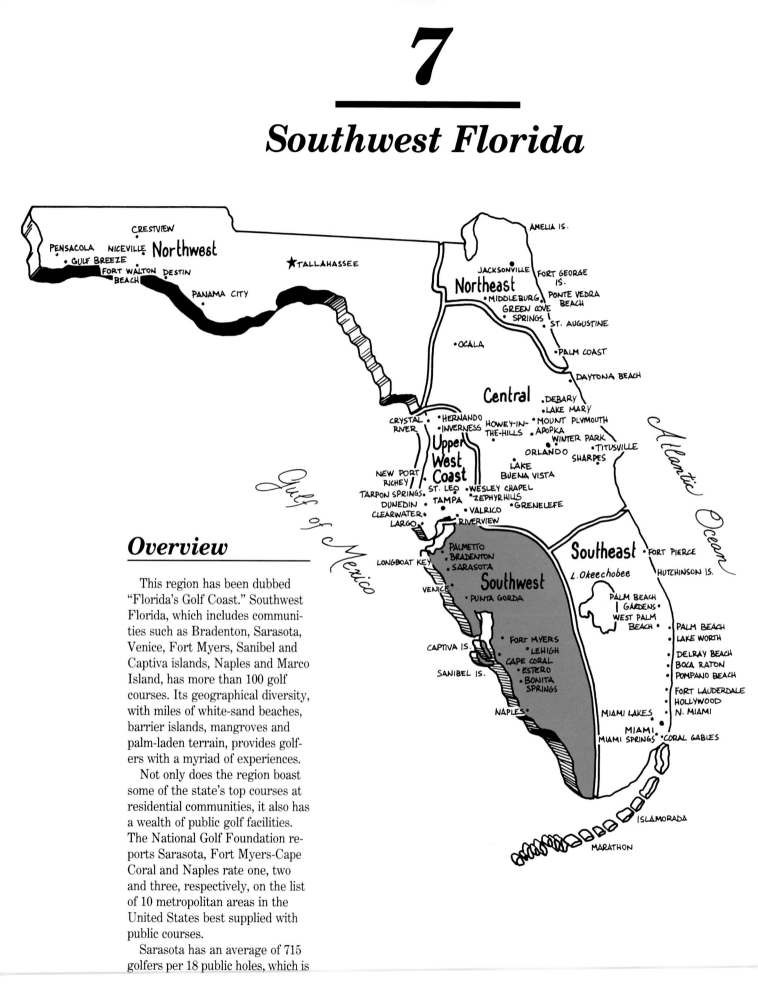

Overview

This region has been dubbed "Florida's Golf Coast." Southwest Florida, which includes communities such as Bradenton, Sarasota, Venice, Fort Myers, Sanibel and Captiva islands, Naples and Marco Island, has more than 100 golf courses. Its geographical diversity, with miles of white-sand beaches, barrier islands, mangroves and palm-laden terrain, provides golfers with a myriad of experiences.

Not only does the region boast some of the state's top courses at residential communities, it also has a wealth of public golf facilities. The National Golf Foundation reports Sarasota, Fort Myers-Cape Coral and Naples rate one, two and three, respectively, on the list of 10 metropolitan areas in the United States best supplied with public courses.

Sarasota has an average of 715 golfers per 18 public holes, which is

astonishing compared with the national average of 3,677 per 18 holes, according to NGF statistics. Better still, the public courses are challenging and designed by such architects as Donald Ross, Arthur Hills and Ron Garl.

Southwest Florida is indeed one of the state's golf meccas. All one has to do is look at the number of PGA and LPGA pros who've associated themselves with golf courses in the region. Fiddlesticks in Fort Myers is the home course for Bobby Nichols, Calvin Peete and Mark Lye. Windstar in Naples has Andy Bean and Nancy Lopez. Ken Venturi lives and works at Eagle Creek in Naples, and Paul Azinger calls River Wilderness in Bradenton home.

For the golf spectator, Southwest Florida features two Senior PGA Tour events. The Aetna Challenge is played each February in Naples. In April, the Senior Tour returns for the Chrysler Cup in Sarasota.

Perhaps the most difficult task when visiting the area is deciding which destinations to select.

Bradenton sports an easy-going lifestyle, uncrowded beaches, many top public golf courses and the convenience of being less than 40 minutes from the Tampa/St. Petersburg area.

Sarasota, down the beach some 13 miles, is an affluent seaside city with the 13th highest per-capita income in the United States. Its cultural offerings attract visitors as much as its golf and beaches. Sarasota also is the birthplace of golf in Florida. In 1885, John Hamilton Gillespie, a homesick Scot, settled in the city and built a two-hole practice course in what is now the downtown business district.

Venice, a city of about 19,000, is laced with canals just like its Italian namesake, and several of its buildings, both private and public, bear a Northern Italian style.

In Fort Myers, a city best known as the beloved winter home of Thomas Edison, immaculately renovated period homes line palm-sheltered boulevards. It might be said that the city is obsessed with golf. Superb golf course communities virtually encircle the city. Fort Myers also is home to four excellent public golf courses.

Located 15 miles southwest of Fort Myers, Sanibel and Captiva islands are reached easily via a modern causeway. The islands are a wonderland of lush tropical foliage framed by the aquamarine waters of the Gulf of Mexico. Often referred to as "Florida's answer to Tahiti," these two islands, where pirates used to roam, offer the quintessential island golf getaway.

Twenty-five miles south of Fort Myers on the famous Tamiami Trail, Naples has been called the Palm Beach of the Southwest Coast of Florida. Fact is, more millionaires per capita live in Naples than Palm Beach, or any other American city. There are more than 100 Fortune 500 executives and some 600 millionaires among Naples residents. Local homeowners include golfer and CBS commentator Ken Venturi, tennis pro Evonne Goolagong, writer Robert Ludlum and *60 Minutes* reporter Mike Wallace. Golf is definitely the sport of choice in Naples as the city has 29 courses to offer.

Marco Island, the largest of Florida's 10,000 islands, is located 16 miles south of Naples. It is home to 10,000 permanent residents, a figure that swells to 25,000 in the winter season.

One of the reasons Southwest Florida is so attractive to golfers is its accessibility. In the past decade the completion of the Interstate 75 extension to Naples and the opening of the Southwest Florida Regional Airport (located 8 miles southeast of Fort Myers) has made the region much easier to visit. Presently, the airport is served by 12 carriers with scheduled service to more than 170 destinations.

The average annual temperature in the region is 73.3 degrees, and it's a foregone conclusion that golf is playable 365 days a year. Winters in Southwest Florida are among the most pleasant anywhere in the continental United States, with temperatures averaging a comfortable 66 degrees. Summers? They're sizzling. However, occasional relief comes from the gentle trade winds that blow year-round off the Gulf of Mexico. Like elsewhere in Florida, when the temperatures rise in the summer the greens fees tumble.

Be sure to stock up on the suntan lotion as water sports activities are year-round pleasures in this region. Another favorite pastime is shell collecting on the beaches of Sanibel and Captiva islands, which are considered a shelling paradise.

During March, don't be surprised if you see a major-league baseball player on the golf course. Golf is a favorite pastime of many players while they're in the area for spring training. The Pittsburgh Pirates train in Bradenton, the Chicago White Sox in Sarasota and the Texas Rangers in Port Charlotte.

Longboat Key Club
Longboat Key

Longboat Key, 5 miles west of Sarasota, was discovered more than 400 years ago by the Spanish explorer Hernando DeSoto, who landed with his men in their long-boats in 1539. Today, the island, encircled by the emerald waters of the Gulf of Mexico, is an elegant resort environment.

Taking advantage of a wide, sug-ar-white quartz sand beach that provides a striking backdrop, the Islandside Course is beautiful and challenging. The course, set on the 1,000-acre resort, is bordered on the west by the Gulf of Mexico and on the east by Sarasota Bay. De-signed by Billy Mitchell and opened for play in 1960, this 6,890-yard, par-72 course winds through 5,000 palm trees and many water hazards. The sinuous fairways thread throughout lakes and la-goons making the layout an ac-knowledged test of accuracy. Wa-ter comes into play on every hole. The ever-present Gulf breezes are a hazard themselves and have blown many tee shots into the wa-ter.

Longboat Key Club, accessible via a causeway from Sarasota, is a private club and residential com-munity. The 222-unit Inn on the Beach offers luxurious vacation apartments ranging from guest rooms to spacious two-bedroom suites with deluxe kitchens. Views are magnificent from every unit, with balconies overlooking the Gulf of Mexico or across the many la-goons of the Islandside Course. The resort is situated in a wildlife sanctuary, which makes it an envi-able spot for those who want to get away from the world of clocks and deadlines.

Life at Longboat Key can be as active or as relaxing as one wishes. There are numerous activities to enjoy, including 30 Har-Tru tennis courts, swimming at The Inn's pool, searching for shells along the 12 miles of beach and bicycling or jogging on the Parcours track. In addition, sailboards and sailboats are available for rent at the beach.

The Longboat Key Club marina has a broad array of charter craft available for deep-sea fishing ex-cursions, sailing and power boat-ing. Also, the area includes mari-nas offering daily party boats for dinner cruises or sightseeing.

Longboat Key Club's convenient location near Sarasota enhances the resort experience immensely. Sarasota is a culturally rich com-munity that boasts museums, the-aters and many upscale shopping complexes.

Longboat Key Club

Hole	1	2	3	4	5	6	7	8	9	10	11	12	13	14	15	16	17	18
Yards	400	500	167	354	372	430	515	192	455	415	400	415	490	200	420	400	230	535
Par	4	5	3	4	4	4	5	3	4	4	4	4	5	3	4	4	3	5

Yardage: 6,890; Par: 72

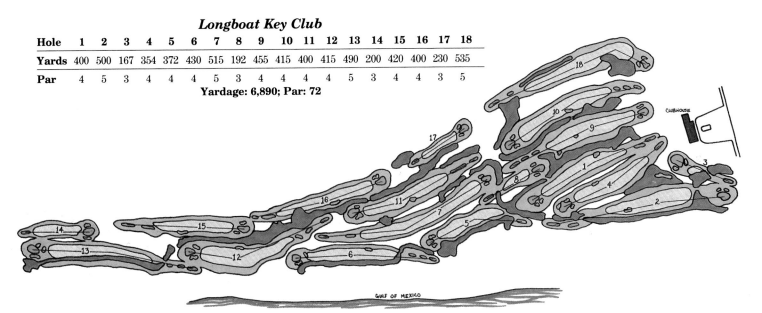

Address: 301 Gulf of Mexico Drive, Longboat Key, Fla. 34228

Phone: (813) 383-8821, (800) 237-8821, in Florida (800) 282-0113

No. of rooms: 222

No. of holes: 18

Sports facilities: tennis, pool, biking and fishing

Restaurants: 2

Business facilities: 5 meeting rooms can accommodate up to 200 people

Location: 5 miles west of Sarasota

Nearby attractions: The Ringling Residence, Ringling Museum of the Circus and shopping at St. Armands Key

South Seas Plantation
Captiva Island

Visitors to Captiva Island bask in a tropical lifestyle that exudes a Caribbean island flavor. Local residents say the most frequent comment from visitors is, "This can't be Florida."

Captiva Island has the legacy of being a secluded enclave to get away from it all. According to legend, the island's natural splendor first caught the attention of pirates seeking sanctuary between raids. During the latter half of the 1700s and into the early 1800s, the many coves and hidden bays of Captiva and adjacent Sanibel Island harbored ships and ragged crews. The name Captiva apparently came about because a pirate named Jose Gaspar kept his women captive here.

The island's birth as a vacation

spot didn't begin until 1900 when Clarence Chadwick, inventor of the checkwriter machine, acquired the

north end of Sanibel and all of Captiva Island.

South Seas Plantation occupies

South Seas Plantation

Hole	1	2	3	4	5	6	7	8	9	10	11	12	13	14	15	16	17	18
Yards	390	415	509	406	559	175	256	112	311	390	415	509	406	559	175	256	112	311
Par	4	4	5	4	5	3	4	3	4	4	4	5	4	5	3	4	3	4

Yardage: 6,266; Par: 72

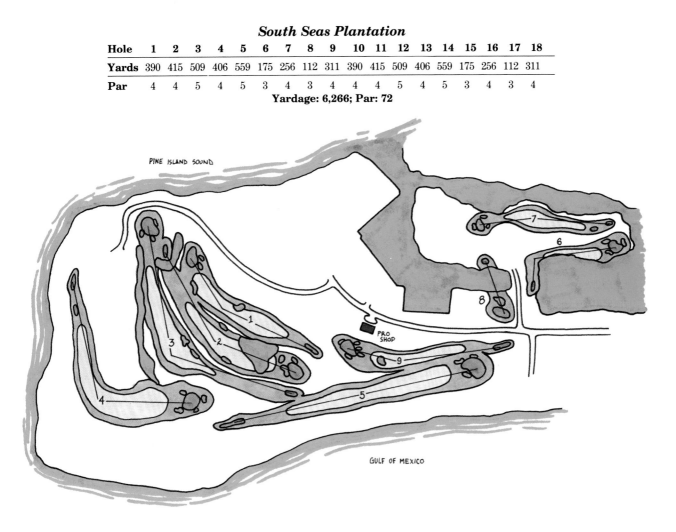

330 acres at the northern tip of Captiva Island (30 miles from Fort Myers). Its 2-mile private beach sets a mood of island tranquility.

The nine-hole, par-36, 3,133-yard course is flat with a couple of lakes and awesome views of the Gulf of Mexico. Quite simply, this is the spot to come if your game is on the skids. Get on the first tee, take a deep breath of the salty air and gaze at the tropical surroundings and you'll forget all about your erratic play. The golf pro shop offers instruction and complete equipment rental. The resident golf director is former PGA touring pro Jerry Heard.

South Seas offers a lot of flexibility in its 600 units available for rent. Among the accommodations available are: Harbourside Village,

deluxe hotel rooms overlooking a yacht harbor; Gulf Cottages, three bedrooms plus loft units with kitchen, living room and two baths; and Land's End Village, two- and three-bedroom units overlooking the golf course and the Gulf.

The water sports recreation menu at South Seas is a lengthy one. It features sailing, wind surfing, fishing, water skiing, scuba diving, rental boats and excursion trips to nearby islands. You'll never be far from a pool — the resort has 15 scattered throughout the property.

Dining at South Seas Plantation ranges from candlelight to casual, and located on Captiva Island are two of Florida's more celebrated restaurants, The Bubble Room and Mucky Duck.

Address: P.O. Box 194, Captiva Island, Fla. 33924
Phone: (813) 472-5111, (800) 237-6000, in Florida (800) 282-6158
No. of rooms: 600
No. of holes: 9
Sports facilities: tennis, 15 pools, charter boat fishing, scuba diving and jet skiing
Restaurants: 3
Business facilities: 27,000-square-foot conference center, 4,000-square-foot Harbourside Meeting Center, can accommodate up to 625
Location: Captiva Island
Nearby attractions: Captain Mike Fuery's Shelling Charters, Cayo Costa Island State Preserve, Cabbage Key

Burnt Store Marina Resort
Punta Gorda

Golfers who share an equal passion for boating will find the Burnt Store Marina Resort, 20 miles north of Fort Myers, offers excellent opportunities to pursue both activities.

The resort has 27 holes of golf, including an 18-hole, 3,850-yard, par-60 course designed by Ron Garl, and a nine-hole, 1,959-yard, par-29 layout designed by Mark McCumber. These short, flat layouts allow for a quick round, which leaves more than ample time to hit the open seas. Be aware, though, these tracts have plenty of water and spray hitters will be on the course a bit longer, engaging, no

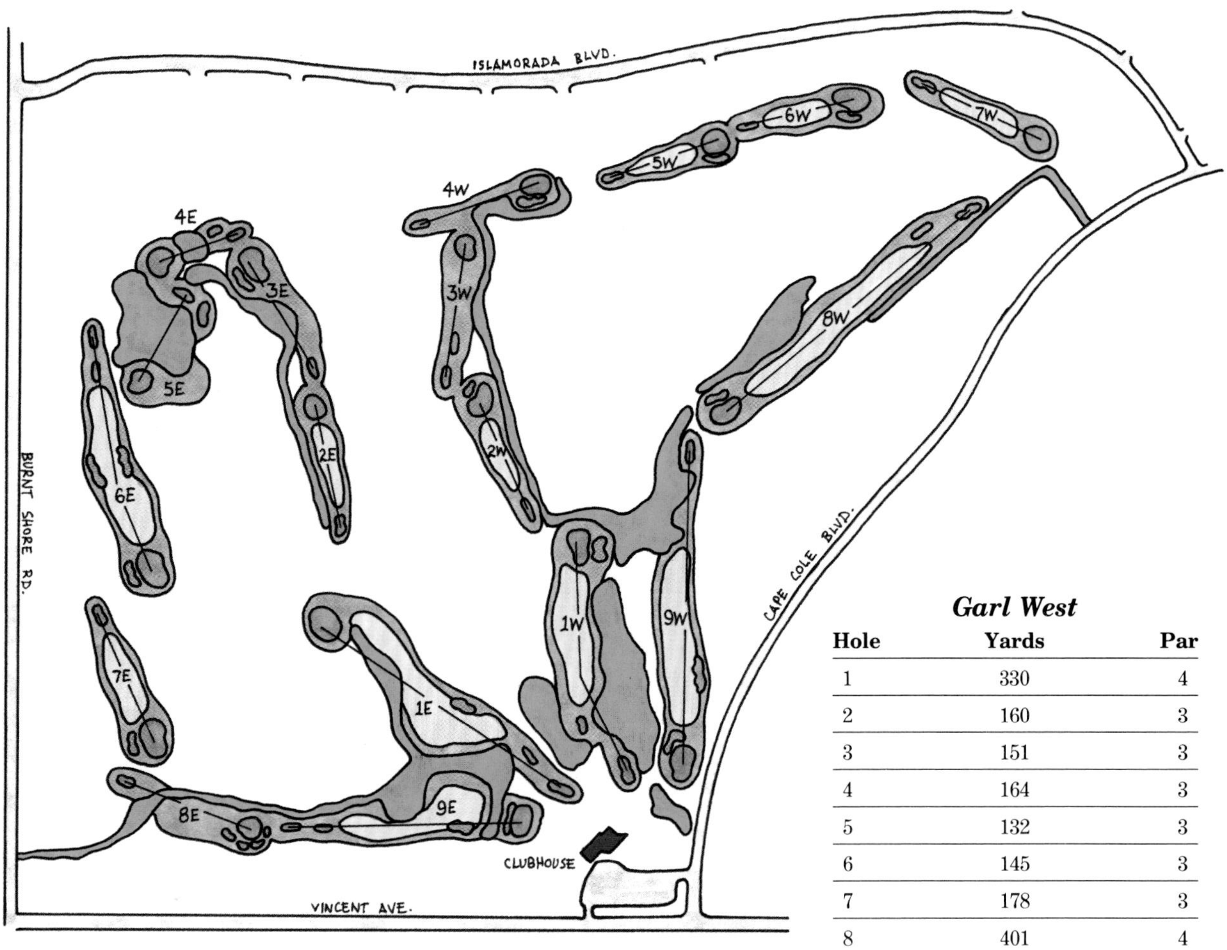
ISLAMORADA BLVD.
BURNT SHORE RD.
CAPE COLE BLVD.
VINCENT AVE.
CLUBHOUSE
1W
2W
3W
4W
5W
6W
7W
8W
9W
1E
2E
3E
4E
5E
6E
7E
8E
9E

Garl West

Hole	Yards	Par
1	330	4
2	160	3
3	151	3
4	164	3
5	132	3
6	145	3
7	178	3
8	401	4
9	379	4
	2,040	**30**

Garl East

Hole	Yards	Par
1	362	4
2	124	3
3	142	3
4	123	3
5	119	3
6	315	4
7	155	3
8	156	3
9	314	4
	1,810	**30**

doubt, in a little "fishing."

The focal point and social activity center for the community is the 425-slip marina that can accommodate vessels up to 70 feet long. Situated in a quiet sheltered cove a few miles from the Gulf of Mexico, the marina is an ideal spot to start a power boat cruise, sailboat outing or deep-sea fishing excursion. Minutes away are exotic and picturesque spots like Cayo Costa, Pine Island and Boca Grande.

For landlubbers who would like to learn how to sail, the resort features the International Sailing School Ltd., which has qualified instructors.

Following a day on the high seas, Salty's Harbourside restaurant, overlooking the marina, has a menu filled with fresh seafood delicacies and some of the best Key Lime pie north of Key West.

The 45-unit Marina Inn provides one-, two- and three-bedroom condominium suites with full-service kitchens, private lanais and smartly appointed living and dining rooms.

Address: 3150 Matecumbe Key Road, Punta Gorda, Fla. 33955

Phone: (800) 237-4255, in Florida (800) 237-1140

No. of rooms: 45

No. of holes: 27

Sports facilities: tennis, bicycling and boating

Restaurants: 1

Business facilities: conference center can accommodate up to 300 people; 4 meeting rooms

Location: Charlotte Harbor, just west of Interstate 75

Nearby attractions: deep-sea fishing, Boca Grande Island excursions

Naples Beach Hotel & Golf Club
Naples

To say that the Naples Beach Hotel & Golf Club is ideally situated for a resort golf getaway is an understatement. A chip shot across the street from the front lobby is the 18-hole championship golf course, and the back of the hotel is fringed by 1,000 feet of sandy Gulf of Mexico shoreline.

The resort's 6,462-yard, par-72 course is one of the oldest in Florida and was the first one in the state to play host to a PGA tournament. The course was built in 1930 and redesigned in 1981 by Ron Garl.

Not all of the sand is on the beach behind the hotel, however. The course is well-trapped and Garl has placed them strategically so that a mistake in club selection or an erratic approach shot will cost golfers dearly. An example of Garl's "sandy" design approach is the 398-yard, par-4 finishing hole. Water and out of bounds on the right require good placement of a tee shot. The second shot is over two water hazards to a green surrounded by three bunkers.

Owned and operated for more than 40 years by the Watkins family, the 135-acre Naples Beach Hotel and Golf Club is the type of sophisticated yet folksy resort that once dominated Florida's coasts before high-rise condos and major hotel chains arrived. It is a resort that pays heed to Old Florida, yet it constantly has been updated to assure quality and luxury.

The 315-room hotel features 56 one-bedroom suites and 50 efficiencies with views of the Gulf or golf course.

Aside from tennis and a host of water sports, one of the more popular pastimes is shopping at the chic boutiques and galleries in downtown Naples — only 5 minutes away via a charming trolley.

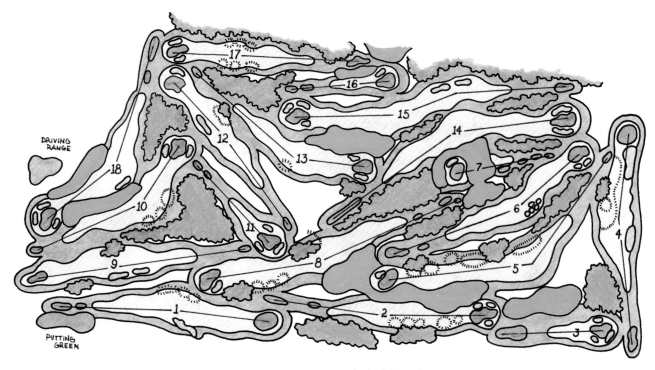

Naples Beach Hotel & Golf Club

Hole	1	2	3	4	5	6	7	8	9	10	11	12	13	14	15	16	17	18
Yards	380	387	187	370	518	401	166	487	361	317	174	362	371	501	523	199	360	398
Par	4	4	3	4	5	4	3	5	4	4	3	4	4	5	5	3	4	4

Yardage: 6,462; Par: 72

Address: 851 Gulf Shores Blvd. N., Naples, Fla. 33940

Phone: (813) 261-2222, (800) 237-7600, in Florida (800) 282-7601

No. of rooms: 315

No. of holes: 18

Sports facilities: tennis, pool, bicycle rental

Restaurants: 3

Business facilities: 7,000 square feet of meeting space with 8 meeting rooms

Location: 5 minutes from downtown Naples

Nearby attractions: Jungle Larry's African Safari Park, Naples Pier and Collier Automotive Museum

Sundial Beach and Tennis Resort
Sanibel Island

Don't let the name fool you, there's a lot of good golf available to guests at this resort. Guests are accorded playing privileges and reduced greens fees at the Dunes Golf and Tennis Club, located about five minutes from the resort. The Dunes is owned by Marquis Hotels, which also owns the Sundial.

"Water, water everywhere" is a good way to describe this 18-hole course on Sanibel Island, 15 miles southwest of Fort Myers. Golf architect Mark McCumber has incorporated water hazards on 16 holes. It's a good idea to bring a few extra balls because even low-handicappers are liable to lose a few here.

The 5,715-yard, par-70 layout tests accuracy and concentration, however, it never lets the golfer lose sight of fun. The most chal-

lenging hole is the 18th, a 459-yard par 5, where it's necessary to hit a long and accurate drive so you can gamble with an approach shot over the water.

Complementing the golf experience is the magnificent island vegetation and the egrets, ospreys

and herons that find the water hazards more accommodating than the golfers do.

The oceanside Sundial Resort has five pools, tennis courts, boats and sailboards and other water sports equipment. Sundial features more than 225 deluxe suites, the

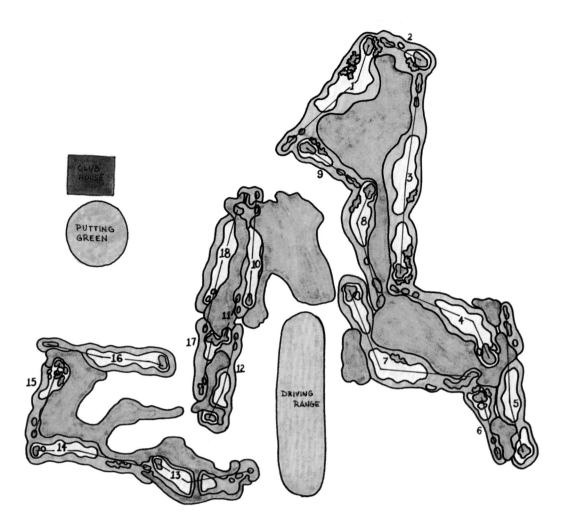

The Dunes Golf & Tennis Club

Hole	1	2	3	4	5	6	7	8	9	10	11	12	13	14	15	16	17	18
Yards	337	101	462	301	355	159	413	302	137	410	172	321	384	442	282	478	200	459
Par	4	3	5	4	4	3	4	4	3	4	3	4	4	4	4	5	3	5

Yardage: 5,715; Par: 70

majority of which have private, screened balconies overlooking landscaped courtyards and the Gulf of Mexico. Guests choose either a one- or two-bedroom unit featuring fully equipped kitchens.

Windows on the Water is an appropriate name for Sundial's featured restaurant, which affords visitors panoramic views of the Gulf.

Two pastimes — bicycling and shell collecting — are highly recommended on Sanibel Island. Bike paths weave around much of the island, allowing cyclists to soak up the tropical scenery. The beaches of this barrier island are among

the best shelling areas in the world. There are no offshore reefs to break up the shells, and the

island's geographical position creates a netlike effect that catches and holds the shells.

Address: 1451 Middle Gulf Drive, Sanibel Island, Fla. 33957
Phone: (800) 237-4184, (813) 472-4151
No. of rooms: 225
No. of holes: 18
Sports facilities: tennis, pools, bicycle paths and water sports equipment rental
Restaurants: 3
Business facilities: 10,000

square feet of meeting space, can handle groups up to 250
Location: Sanibel Island, 15 miles southwest of Fort Myers via causeway.
Nearby attractions: J.N. "Ding" Darling National Wildlife Refuge on Sanibel Island, shopping on Periwinkle Way on Sanibel Island, Thomas Edison's winter home and laboratory in Fort Myers

Plantation Golf & Country Club
Venice

With its pastel-tinted homes appointed with white-tiled roofs, lattice accents and white shutters, and lushly landscaped boulevards, the Plantation is reminiscent of the simple, understated elegance of Bermuda. Located just south of Venice on U.S. Highway 41, the Plantation Golf & Country Club is a 1,300-acre residential/resort community of condominiums, villas and single-family homes.

The Plantation's two 18-hole championship courses, The Bobcat and The Panther, were designed by Ron Garl and are highly rated

and challenging. Duffers will find these courses playable, and touring pros will find them a superb test of skill. The LPGA stages the Second Regional Qualifier and the National Teaching Division Championship annually at the Plantation.

Measuring 6,862 yards, the par-72 Bobcat features numerous lakes and rolling hills. Water surrounds 16 holes, and on 12 holes the green is not visible from the tee. Garl: "It's best to take your time at the tee and carefully determine your landing area target. Those swinging for the fences, so to speak, will

be cussing me out a lot."

Completed in 1987, the 6,307-yard, par-72 Panther course showcases two spectacular island greens and Scottish-type fairways. The Panther also features rolling hills, tiered greens and elevated landing areas.

There are many nature preserve areas in and around the courses, and the golf experience is enhanced by the beautiful scenery and wildlife, such as herons, egrets and raccoons that roam the course.

The centerpiece of the Plantation is its Bermuda-style clubhouse

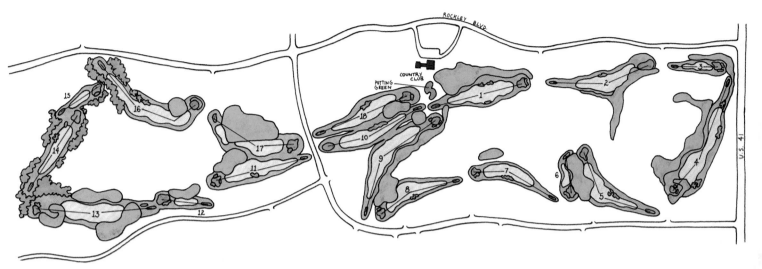

The Bobcat

Hole	1	2	3	4	5	6	7	8	9	10	11	12	13	14	15	16	17	18
Yards	396	422	184	537	437	158	397	364	538	425	401	193	530	373	180	513	392	422
Par	4	4	3	5	4	3	4	4	5	4	4	3	5	4	3	5	4	4

Yardage: 6,862; Par: 72

overlooking the Bobcat course's first hole and practice green. The clubhouse complex includes a junior Olympic-size pool, nine lighted tennis courts, and The Manor Restaurant, which serves continental cuisine to members and the public.

Anglers also enjoy the Plantation and its 45 acres of interconnected lakes, which are stocked with largemouth bass, bluegill, speckled perch and catfish.

The Plantation's resort rental program manages about 200 privately owned two- and three-bedroom garden residences and condominiums for weekend, weekly or monthly rentals.

Address: 500 Rockley Blvd., Venice, Fla. 34293
Phone: (800) 826-4060, (813) 493-2146, (813) 493-2500
No. of rooms: 200
No. of holes: 36
Sports facilities: tennis, fitness trail, biking and pools
Restaurants: 2
Business facilities: small meeting rooms in clubhouse
Location: Venice area
Nearby attractions: Gulf coast beaches, shopping in Venice

Lehigh Resort
Lehigh

Nestled amid a wide expanse of Southwest Florida flatland populated with palms, oaks, and pines 12 miles east of Fort Myers, the Lehigh Resort is a family-oriented vacation getaway with two 18-hole golf courses.

Bordering the resort facilities, the North Course measures 6,459 yards and plays to a par 71. The tree-lined fairways are narrow and the greens are small. Prevailing winds and water add to the challenge. One of the more harrowing

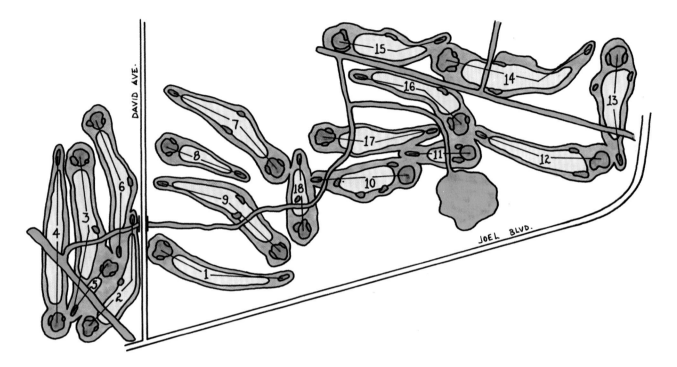

Lehigh Golf Club

Hole	1	2	3	4	5	6	7	8	9	10	11	12	13	14	15	16	17	18
Yards	374	341	440	511	171	410	404	201	432	320	167	530	360	513	356	341	412	176
Par	4	4	4	5	3	4	4	3	4	4	3	5	4	5	4	4	4	3

Yardage: 6,459; Par: 71

holes is No. 15, a 356-yard par 4 that has the entire left side bordered by a canal with approach shots to a well-bunkered and contoured green.

Minutes away from the resort, the 6,490-yard, par-72 South Course is more open than its counterpart. Big hitters will like this layout because of its wide fairways and generous landing areas.

Guests staying at the 154-unit resort stay at the two-story motel complex or villas. Standard motel rooms, efficiencies, and one- and two-bedroom units are available.

Recreational amenities include a pool, four lighted tennis courts, shuffleboard, volleyball and freshwater fishing. Arrangements also can be made through the resort for deep-sea fishing excursions in the Gulf of Mexico (35 miles away).

Fresh Florida seafood is prepared to perfection at 255 East, Lehigh's fine dining restaurant.

Address: 225 East Joel Blvd., Lehigh, Fla. 33936
Phone: (813) 369-2121, (800) 843-0971, in Florida (800) 237-2251
No. of rooms: 154
No. of holes: 36
Sports facilities: tennis, volleyball, fishing, pool
Restaurants: 1
Business facilities: 7,500 square feet of meeting space, can handle groups up to 200
Location: on Route 884, 12 miles east of Fort Myers
Nearby attractions: The Everglades, Edison Winter Home and Fort Myers Historical Museum

Best Of The Rest

Perhaps no other area in the nation has as many top-notch public golf facilities as Southwest Florida. Chances are, after playing the region's best public courses, you'll forget the notion that public and municipal courses belong at the bottom of any rating list.

The Manatee County-owned Buffalo Creek course, a 7,000-yard, par-72 layout designed by Ron Garl is in as good a condition as most private clubs. The Scottish-links-type course is challenging but playable with no water-lined fairways and no traps in front of any greens.

Two public courses in the Fort Myers area that are highly ranked in national and regional golf publications are the Robert Von Hagge-Bruce Devlin-designed Eastwood Golf Course (6,772 yards, par 72) and the 6,937-yard, par-72 Pelican's Nest in Bonita Springs, which was designed by Tom Fazio.

In Cape Coral, just north of Fort Myers, Coral Oaks is an exceptional public course designed by Arthur Hills. Thick stands of tall Florida pine and stately oak trees provide beauty and hazards on the 6,645-yard, par-72 layout.

For Dick Wilson design fans, the Golden Gate Country Club course in Naples is a superb 6,630-yard, par-72 test of skill.

Buffalo Creek (public)
Route 5, Box OS
Palmetto, Fla. 33561
(904) 776-2611
18 holes

Eastwood Country Club (public)
4600 Bruce Herd Lane
Fort Myers, Fla. 33905
(813) 332-2327
18 holes

Pelican's Nest Golf Club (resort)
4450 Bay Creek Drive SW
Bonita Springs, Fla. 33923
(813) 947-4600
18 holes

Coral Oaks Golf Club (public)
1800 NW 28th Ave.
Cape Coral, Fla. 33909
(813) 283-4100
18 holes

Golden Gate Golf Club
(semiprivate)
4100 Golden Gate Parkway
Naples, Fla. 33999
(813) 455-1010
18 holes

Other Courses To Consider

Bobby Jones Golf Club (public)
1000 Circus Blvd.
Sarasota, Fla. 34232
(813) 955-8097
45 holes

Foxfire Golf Club (semiprivate)
7200 Proctor Road
Sarasota, Fla. 34241
(813) 921-7757
54 holes

Gateway Golf Club (semiprivate)
Gateway Blvd.
Fort Myers, Fla. 33907
(813) 947-4600
18 holes

Manatee County Golf Club (public)
5290 66th St. W.
Bradenton, Fla. 33507
(813) 792-6773
18 holes

The Meadows (semiprivate)
3103 Longmeadow
Sarasota, Fla. 34235
(813) 378-6650
54 holes

River's Edge Yacht & Country Club (semiprivate)
14700 Portsmouth Blvd. SW
Fort Myers, Fla. 33908
(813) 433-4211
18 holes

Wildcat Run (semiprivate)
20300 Country Club Drive
Estero, Fla. 33928
(813) 463-7558
18 holes

Oak Ford (semiprivate)
1552 Palm View Road
Sarasota, Fla. 34240
(813) 371-3680
27 holes

Tatum Ridge (public)
421 North Tatum Road
Sarasota, Fla. 34240
(813) 378-4211
18 holes

8

Southeast Florida

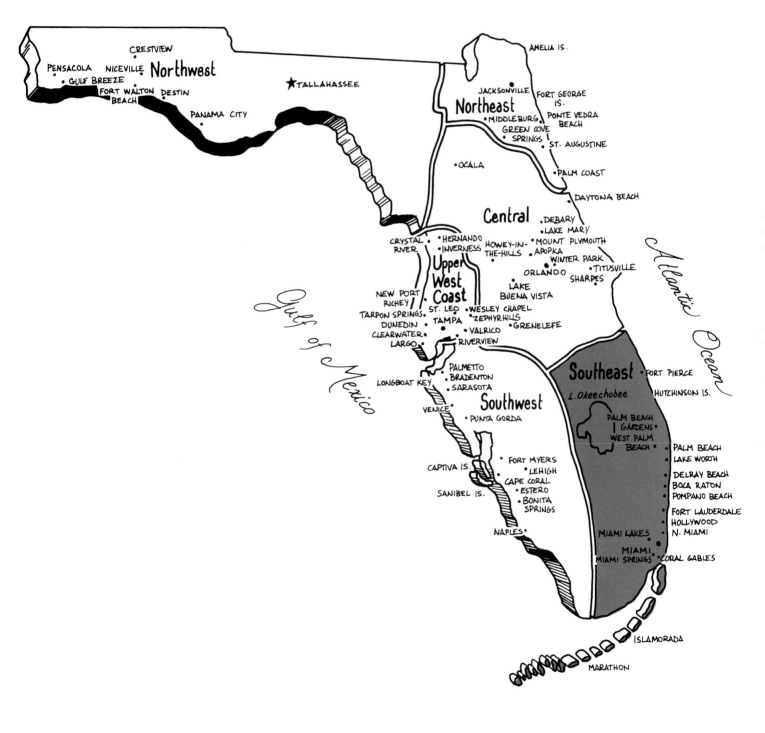

Overview

Many golfers look to this tropical region for the quintessential Florida golf experience. Fringed by miles and miles of Atlantic Ocean beach, Southeast Florida offers a variety of resort lifestyles from the ultra-wealthy ambience of Palm Beach and Boca Raton to the sun-and-fun atmosphere in Fort Lauderdale to the international glitz of Miami to the laid-back appeal of the Florida Keys.

Miami

Turnberry Isle

Golf has been a strong magnet for visitors to the area since the early 1900s. Henry Flagler, the railroad magnate responsible for building the railroad that opened up the state to tourists from the North, built six of the first eight golf courses in Florida. Ironically, Flagler was not a golfer and actually thought the game to be a frivolous waste of time. He reasoned, however, that guests desired to be pampered with many amenities at their hotels. Other hotels followed his lead, and this region now has several of the nation's legendary resort hotels, which feature golf as their main attraction.

The city of Palm Beach, with its steady stream of wealthy celebrity visitors, is recognized as one of the nation's ritziest communities.

Many people are unaware, however, that Palm Beach County offers a wide range of hotel options (ranging from five-star deluxe to economy) in such cities as West Palm Beach, Palm Beach Gardens, Jupiter and Boca Raton — as well as pricey Palm Beach itself. Palm Beach Gardens, site of the headquarters of the Professional Golfers Association, has been referred to as the "capital of American golf." Golf course architects who have designed in Palm Beach County include Jack Nicklaus, Pete Dye, Arthur Hills, Tom Fazio and Ron Garl.

Fort Lauderdale is no longer the suds-and-sun spring break haven for college students. City officials made a decision to transform the area to a destination for families, young professionals and meeting

Miami Lakes Inn

Doral Resort and Country Club

groups. There are more than 50 golf courses in Broward County, which includes high-profile municipalities such as Fort Lauderdale, Deerfield Beach, Hallandale, Hollywood, Lauderdale-By-The-Sea and Pompano Beach.

Despite its well-documented problems, Miami remains a world-class destination offering a myriad of vacation experiences — year-round outdoor sports, fine dining, shopping, museums, concerts and special events.

If your image of a Florida golf vacation is swaying palms, white sand traps, carpetlike fairways and soft sea breezes, then chances are you're thinking of the more than 20 golf courses in the Miami area.

Golf in the Keys is limited to only a few layouts, but it's still the ideal spot for those who want to combine sport fishing and golf during a getaway. Islamorada, a 16-mile island chain within a chain, is considered by some the sport fish-

Florida Keys

ing capital of the world. The golf courses in the Keys make up for their generally unchallenging designs with picturesque settings.

This region's climate is tropical with an average year-round temperature in the mid-70s. If you're on a Southeast Florida golf course in July, August or September, be

prepared for an afternoon drenching from the predictable daily rains. Because of its closeness to the equator, this region more than any other in Florida has comfortable temperatures year-round, with no more than a dozen days a year where temperatures might dip below 60 degrees.

Besides beach activities, boating, tennis and sightseeing, this region offers some of the best fishing in the continental United States. For example, Broward County is one of the few areas in the world where both freshwater and saltwater fishing are within 20 minutes. Miami and the Keys also are located near prime off-shore fishing grounds.

It is one of the state's most accessible regions with hundreds of flights daily into Miami International Airport, Fort Lauderdale-/Hollywood International Airport and Palm Beach International Airport. The Keys have two airports, one in Key West and the other in Marathon.

The Breakers
Palm Beach

Since the 1920s the champagne and caviar set have pursued the opulent Palm Beach lifestyle at The Breakers. Designed by Leonard Schultze of Waldorf Astoria fame, the huge, seven-story edifice with its strong Italian Renaissance flavor still is the society center of Palm Beach.

The architectural design of the exterior of the hotel, with its twin belvedere towers and graceful arches, was inspired by the famous Villa Medici in Florence. The Florentine fountain in front of the hotel is patterned after the one in the Boboli Gardens in Florence. If you don't have the time or inclination to travel to Europe for a golf getaway, the Breakers is overflowing with European ambience.

Fortunately, the hotel has not blinded itself to the 1990s, and it offers a full range of recreation amenities and children's programs, which help to attract a younger and more active clientele.

The Breakers Hotel and its related facilities are set on 140 acres of beachfront property. A chip shot away from the main lobby is the

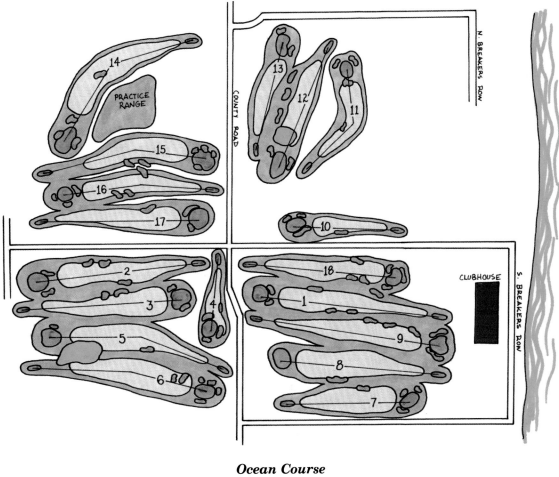

Ocean Course

Hole	1	2	3	4	5	6	7	8	9	10	11	12	13	14	15	16	17	18
Yards	348	356	350	125	370	398	297	301	379	200	356	393	225	460	353	349	349	347
Par	4	4	4	3	4	5	4	4	4	3	4	5	3	5	4	4	4	4

Yardage: 5,956; Par: 70

Donald Ross-designed Ocean Course, one of Florida's oldest courses. Only 5,956 yards and a par of 70, the Ocean Course has tight fairways and small elevated greens. When the wind blows heartily off the Atlantic Ocean the course becomes dramatically more difficult.

The Breakers West championship course, a 25-minute drive from the hotel (complimentary transportation provided), is a 7,101-yard, relatively flat layout that originally was designed by Willard Byrd in 1968. It recently has been updated by golf course architect Joe Lee.

In between the pampering one receives at the Breakers — the hotel has a 1,200 member staff for a guest-to-staff ratio rivaling a cruise ship — guests can engage in a long list of recreational pursuits. A heated Olympic-size pool, 19 tennis courts, two croquet courts, a half-mile private beach, fitness center and bicycling and jogging trail are among the many activities available.

The Breaker's 528 richly appointed rooms, which recently have been renovated, offer guests a choice of ocean, fairway or garden views.

Address: 1 South County Road, Palm Beach, Fla. 33480
Phone: (407) 659-8440, (800) 833-3141
No. of rooms: 528
No. of holes: 36
Sports facilities: tennis, fitness center, croquet, pool, snorkeling and scuba diving
Restaurants: 5
Business facilities: 32,000 square feet of meeting space
Location: Island of Palm Beach
Nearby attractions: Flagler Museum, Norton Gallery and School of Art, Worth Avenue Shopping and Lion Country Safari

Palm Beach Polo & Country Club
West Palm Beach

One thing is for sure at the Palm Beach Polo and Country Club, if your golf game goes on the blink, you'll have little trouble riding off into the sunset. The 2,200-acre luxury residential/resort community combines 45 holes of championship golf with a $12 million Equestrian Center and various other first-class amenities.

Palm Beach Polo's golf holes were designed by a virtual who's who lineup of golf course architects, including Pete and P.B. Dye, Ron Garl and Jerry Pate and Tom and George Fazio.

Mention the name Pete Dye to golfers and more than a few will

purchase an extra dozen balls before taking on one of his layouts. Dye has designed some of the nation's toughest courses. His 7,116-yard, par-72 Cypress Course at Palm Beach Polo is vintage Dye

(with help from his son P.B.) with hallmark features such as abrupt drop-offs around bunkers and mounds, huge bunkers paralleling lakes and blind shots. One of the more intriguing holes is the 376-

Dunes Course

Hole	1	2	3	4	5	6	7	8	9	10	11	12	13	14	15	16	17	18
Yards	422	331	532	398	198	450	547	180	415	394	544	455	234	374	194	410	531	441
Par	4	4	5	4	3	4	5	3	4	4	5	4	3	4	3	4	5	4

Yardage: 7,050; Par: 72

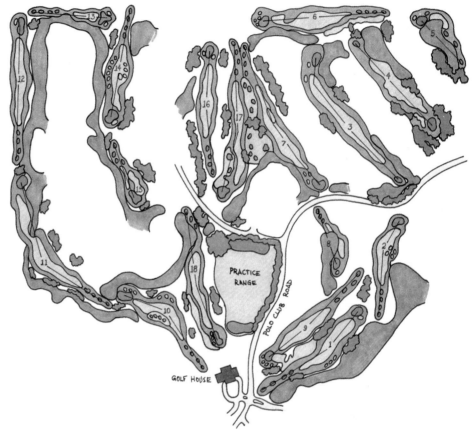

yard, par-4 14th that carries over a lake to a landing area with a cypress tree in the center of the fairway. From there, it's "target golf" to an elevated green.

Challenging golf at Palm Beach Polo doesn't end with Dye's design, either. The Dunes Course (7,050 yards, par 72) is a Scottish links design with its own reputation for intimidation. Lakeland architect Ron Garl and former U.S. Open champion Jerry Pate built the Scottish look-alike course with extensive mounding, pot bunkers, grass traps and fairways full of ripples and swales.

The resort also has a nine-hole course designed by George and Tom Fazio.

For horse fanciers, Palm Beach Polo's Equestrian Center is one of the nation's most comprehensive facilities with three cooperative barns, one show barn and a grand prix ring. Palm Beach Polo is home of the prestigious Winter Equestrian Festival circuit, which features three grand prix events, one of which is a World Cup-qualifying event. More than 1,500 horses valued in excess of $150 million annually compete in this festival.

Polo fans will find 10 fields where top tournaments are staged each winter.

Other sports activities include tennis (20 clay, two grass and two hard courts) and croquet.

Guest lodging is clustered around, or adjacent to, one of the resort's sports facilities: golf, polo or tennis. One- and two-story villas offer 130 units including one-, two- and three-bedroom suites and studios.

Address: 13198 Forest Hill Blvd., West Palm Beach, Fla. 33414
Phone: (407) 798-7000, (800) 327-4204, in Florida (800) 432-4151
No. of rooms: 130
No. of holes: 45
Sports facilities: tennis, croquet, health club, polo, squash and racquetball
Restaurants: 5
Business facilities: 6,000 square feet of meeting space
Location: West Palm Beach area
Nearby attractions: Worth Avenue Shopping in Palm Beach, Palm Beach Opera, Royal Poinciana Playhouse

Boca Raton Resort and Club
Boca Raton

The orange-pink stucco Cloister, surrounded by towering palm trees conjures up images of French Riviera opulence. Built in 1926 by eccentric, self-taught architect Addison Mizner, the Cloister, looking like a combination castle and fortress, is Spanish-Moorish in style and gives visitors an idea of what early Florida was like. The Boca Raton Hotel and Club in Boca Raton long has been recognized as one of the nation's most exclusive golf getaways.

Gerald Ford, Frank Sinatra and Phil Harris have played the 6,682-yard, par-71 course that winds through a resort estate. The course originally was designed by William Flynn in 1926, redesigned in 1956 by Robert Trent Jones and again in 1988 by Joe Lee. Among the modifications made by Lee were the addition of one lake, reshaping traps, completely rebuilding seven holes and new grass on all greens and fairways.

Former pros at the resort include Tommy Armour from 1926-1955 and Sam Snead between 1956 and 1970. Ron Polane, Boca's executive golf professional, joined the Boca staff as resident pro and first assistant to Snead in 1963.

Golfing privileges also are available at the Boca Raton Golf and Tennis Country Club (15 minutes away by shuttle), which features an 18-hole course designed by Lee.

The atmosphere at the Boca, as regulars affectionately call it, is unmistakably affluent. It's a good idea to take along your best golf attire. Most golfers at the Boca look as if they just stepped out of a high-fashion golf magazine.

The hotel consists of four distinct sections: The 387-room Cloister, with its flower and fountain-laden courtyards and Old Florida ambience; the 242-room Tower, a modern 27-story building that affords sweeping views of the Atlantic Ocean; the secluded Golf Villas, 120 guest rooms and apartments set on the golf course; and the seaside Boca Beach Club with its 214 rooms and seven suites.

While you're there, explore the Mizner Museum where you'll walk past giant columns of a 13th century loggia and view antiques brought from Spain by Mizner.

The Health Club includes an exercise room, whirlpool, massage and a variety of aerobic and aquatic exercise classes. Water enthusiasts can take a free boat ride to the Beach Club where boating, sailing, water-skiing, windsurfing, snorkeling and scuba lessons are available. Arrangements can be made for deep-sea fishing and drift fishing. Tennis players will find 29 clay courts.

Boca Raton Resort and Club

Hole	1	2	3	4	5	6	7	8	9	10	11	12	13	14	15	16	17	18
Yards	387	324	398	164	536	422	429	178	598	553	375	167	573	421	187	374	151	445
Par	4	4	4	3	5	4	4	3	5	5	4	3	5	4	3	4	3	4

Yardage: 6,682; Par: 71

Address: 501 E. Camino Real, Boca Raton, Fla. 33431-0825
Phone: (407) 395-3000, (800) 327-0101
No. of rooms: 965
No. of holes: 36
Sports facilities: fitness center, swimming, tennis, charter fishing, croquet and volleyball
Restaurants: 8
Business facilities: 65,000 square feet of meeting facilities with 29 meeting rooms to accommodate groups up to 1,500 people
Location: Boca Raton
Nearby attractions: Town Centre Shopping Mall, Mizner Tour, Polo from January through April

Sheraton Bonaventure Resort & Spa
Fort Lauderdale

What could Zsa Zsa Gabor, Eddie Murphy and Neil Diamond possibly have in common? They've all been guests at the Sheraton Bonaventure Resort and Spa.

Situated in the 1,250-acre Bonaventure residential community, the resort attracts celebrities and non-celebrities with a deluxe 504-room hotel, gourmet dining, world famous spa and two 18-hole golf courses.

The Spa, encompassing more than 43,000 square feet, is a wonderland of saunas, steam rooms, plunge pools and sun decks with an emphasis on nutrition and stress reduction.

One resident physician and three nurses are on staff to provide complete medical examinations and laboratory tests to determine individually planned exercise programs.

The challenging golf at the Bonaventure might increase your stress level so the Spa is indeed a welcome amenity. Designed by Joe Lee, the 7,011-yard, par-72 Cascades Course is known for its picturesque 160-yard, par-3 waterfall hole. A bit less demanding and shorter in length is the 6,189-yard, par-70 Champions Course, designed by Charlie Mahanna.

From September through April, Bonaventure plays host to John Jacobs Golf School. Jacobs provides weeklong instruction (Monday through Friday) for interested parties at all levels of play. Group clinics for resort guests at the beginner, intermediate and advanced levels can be arranged by Bonaventure's teaching professionals, as well.

Few resorts can match the Bonaventure's seemingly endless lineup of recreation amenities, which include a roller skating rink, tennis, racquetball, squash, horseback riding, bowling and more.

Cascades Course

Hole	Yards	Par
1	563	5
2	349	4
3	160	3
4	430	4
5	391	4
6	177	3
7	540	5
8	415	4
9	429	4
10	540	5
11	427	4
12	181	3
13	403	4
14	430	4
15	388	4
16	579	5
17	179	3
18	430	4
	7,011	**72**

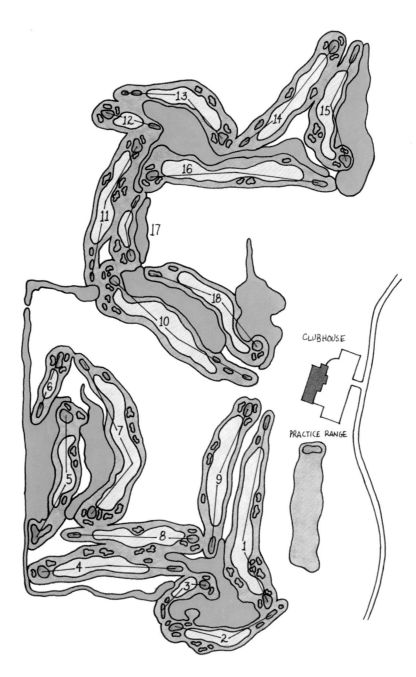

Address: 250 Racquet Club Road, Fort Lauderdale, Fla. 33326

Phone: (305) 389-3300, (800) 327-8090

No. of rooms: 504

No. of holes: 36

Sports facilities: tennis, racquetball, squash, horseback riding

Restaurants: 6

Business facilities: 85,000-square-foot conference center

Location: Fort Lauderdale area

Nearby attractions: Six Flags Atlantis, Butterfly World, Ocean World

Turnberry Isle Yacht & Country Club
North Miami

Set on a private 300-acre island on the Intracoastal Waterway in the exclusive Aventura area of North Miami, Turnberry, with two courses designed by master golf course architect Robert Trent Jones, has little trouble attracting golfers seeking seclusion and challenge. Adding to the resort's golf magnetism is Director of Golf and Touring Professional Raymond Floyd, former U.S. Open and Masters' Tournament champion whose illustrious career includes 21 PGA Tour titles.

Waterways wind gracefully through the courses, which are impeccably maintained. The South Course measures 7,003 yards and plays to a par 72; the North Course is 6,323 yards and is a par 70.

The Mediterranean-inspired architecture of the resort's main structures combined with the secluded location makes you feel as though you're staying at some trendy, isolated European hideaway. Turnberrry Isle has every-

thing a golfer in search of an all-pampering golf getaway might want. There are 24 tennis courts, three pro shops, a spa and health center, marina, private beach club and five restaurants.

The resort is undergoing a $67 million expansion program set for completion in late 1990. It will add additional guest rooms, suites and meeting facilities.

Attention seaworthy golfers, boat owners can dock at Turnberry Isle, where the marina has 117

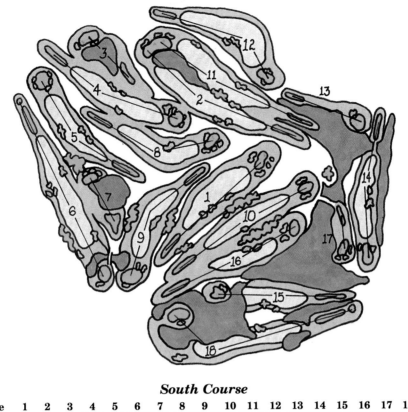

South Course

Hole	1	2	3	4	5	6	7	8	9	10	11	12	13	14	15	16	17	18
Yards	392	536	208	437	427	539	168	404	412	428	503	406	210	417	411	400	160	545
Par	4	5	3	4	4	5	3	4	4	4	5	4	3	4	4	4	3	5

Yardage: 7,003; Par: 72

slips for boats up to 150 feet. The Yacht Club Hotel has 18 rooms and suites, and the Marina Hotel has 40 rooms and suites, all with views of the Intracoastal Waterway and the marina.

The Country Club Hotel's 119 rooms are appointed with terracotta floors, plush area rugs, blond wood furniture and Italian red marble. French doors open to flower-lined terraces with spectacular views of the golf courses or pool gardens. In late 1990, an additional 112 rooms will complete the guest facilities at Turnberry.

Kayaking, windsurfing and Hobie-Cat sailing are available at the Ocean Club and private lessons are offered for novices.

For shopping enthusiasts, the Aventura Mall, which features upscale stores such as Lord & Taylor and Macy's, is only a short shuttle away from the resort.

Address: 19735 Turnberry Way, Aventura, North Miami, Fla. 33180
Phone: (305) 932-6200, (800) 327-7028
No. of rooms: 238
No. of holes: 36
Sports facilities: tennis, pools, on-site marina, health club and spa
Restaurants: 5
Business facilities: 31,000 square feet of meeting space, Grand Ballroom is 12,000 square feet and can accommodate dinner events for up to 1,000 guests
Location: Aventura section of North Miami
Nearby attractions: deep-sea fishing, Miami Art Deco District, Vizcaya

Palm-Aire Spa Resort
Pompano Beach

Even if your spouse doesn't know a bunker from a bogey, Palm-Aire, with its five golf courses and internationally famous spa, seems the perfect locale for the golf fanatic and golf widow who just happen to be married to each other.

For the fanatic, the golf lineup includes courses designed by golf architects like George Fazio, William Mitchell and Robert von Hagge. The Cypress, which meas-

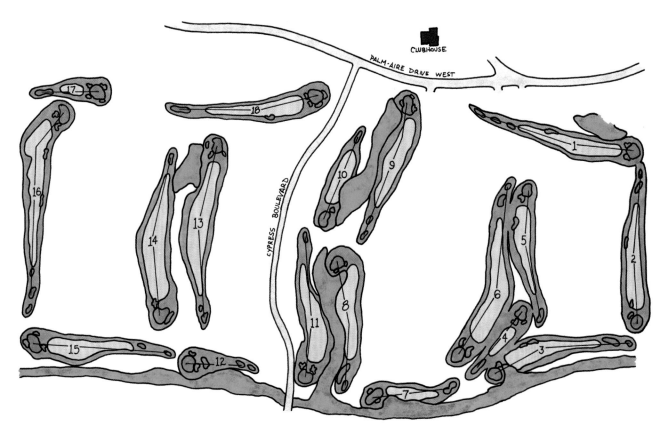

The Cypress

Hole	1	2	3	4	5	6	7	8	9	10	11	12	13	14	15	16	17	18
Yards	553	430	405	220	373	514	225	378	428	145	428	220	505	504	390	582	180	430
Par	5	4	4	3	4	5	3	4	4	3	4	3	5	5	4	5	3	4

Yardage: 6,910; Par: 72

ures 6,910 yards and plays to par 72, is the longest of the five and has large undulating, well-trapped greens and an abundance of palms and Australian pine trees lining its fairways. The resort features 94 holes of golf, including an enjoyable 22-hole executive course ideal for working kinks out of a troublesome iron game.

For the golf widow, Palm-Aire's 55,000-square-foot spa is an oasis of pampering, where guests luxuriate with saunas, massages, facials, herbal wraps and centuries-old techniques of skin and body care. Palm-Aire Spa's customer list includes Elizabeth Taylor, Farrah Fawcett, Liza Minelli and Merv Griffin.

Located midway between Palm Beach and Miami, Palm-Aire is 20 minutes from Fort Lauderdale International Airport. Spread over 700 acres, the resort, which completed an $8 million renovation in 1989, has 191 one- and two-bedroom accommodations, each with a private terrace and many overlooking a golf course.

Besides golf and the spa, the resort offers sports enthusiasts 37 tennis courts, racquetball and squash facilities, a jogging course and fitness and weight training machines.

Address: 2501 Palm-Aire Drive North, Pompano Beach, Fla. 33069
Phone: (305) 968-2700, (800) 336-2108
No. of rooms: 191
No. of holes: 94
Sports facilities: tennis, squash and jogging course
Restaurants: 3
Business facilities: 15,000 square feet of meeting space, can accommodate groups up to 300
Location: Pompano Beach area
Nearby attractions: Six Flags Atlantis, Ocean World, Pompano Harness Track

Diplomat Resort and Country Club
Hollywood

The Diplomat Resort, one of Florida's largest, has an astonishing number of amenities including 12 tennis courts, six restaurants, four lounges, three swimming pools, two health clubs, a marina, and a 1,400-foot-long private beach. Your toughest task might be finding enough time to squeeze in a round of golf.

Designed by Red Lawrence in 1958, the 6,624-yard, par 72 Diplomat Country Club Course is a flat tract with plenty of water hazards and bunkers strategically situated to place a premium on accuracy. Among Lawrence's other designs are the West Course at The Wigwam in Litchfield Park, Ariz., and the Desert Forest in Carefree, Ariz.

One of the Diplomat's more engaging features is its tropical garden, which has 12 waterfalls, rock formations, palm trees and exotic plants encircling a large lagoonlike pool. The entire Diplomat complex (300 acres), in fact, emotes a tropical feel with more than 100 coconut trees and countless shrubs and ferns dotting the property.

The resort long has been a favorite for visiting dignitaries and entertainment stars. At the Celebrity Room, the resort's premier fine dining offering, huge murals of notables like Frank Sinatra, Sammy Davis, Jr. and Kenny Rogers grace the walls.

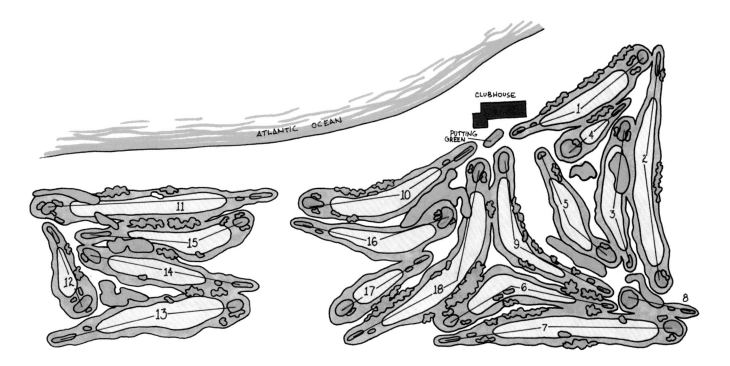

Country Club Golf Course

Hole	1	2	3	4	5	6	7	8	9	10	11	12	13	14	15	16	17	18
Yards	335	555	342	186	351	398	514	165	437	392	497	187	410	372	373	361	226	523
Par	4	5	4	3	4	4	5	3	4	4	5	3	4	4	4	4	3	5

Yardage: 6,624; Par: 72

Situated with the Atlantic Ocean on one side, and the intracoastal waterway on the other, the Diplomat is located less than a half hour from Miami International Airport and 15 minutes from Hollywood-Fort Lauderdale International Airport.

If you love water sports, this is the place for you, with on-the-beach rentals of catamarans, aqua bikes, surfboards, air rafts and snorkel equipment.

The Diplomat offers 1,000 rooms, including 69 suites and 22 pool/oceanside Lanai Rooms as well as a shopping arcade that includes a travel agency, clothing store, barber shop, drug store and florist.

Address: 3515 S. Ocean Drive, Hollywood, Fla. 33022
Phone: (305) 457-8111, (800) 327-1212
No. of rooms: 1,000
No. of holes: 18
Sports facilities: tennis, pools, marina, health club
Restaurants: 6
Business facilities: 100,000 square feet of meeting space with 42 flexible meeting rooms
Location: 15 minutes south of Fort Lauderdale-Hollywood International Airport
Nearby attractions: Hollywood Greyhound Track, Gulfstream Race Track, Dania jai alai, Miami Seaquarium and Ocean World

PGA Sheraton Resort
Palm Beach Gardens

The PGA Sheraton Resort, 20 miles north of Palm Beach, serves as the administrative headquarters of the PGA. Naturally, the courses are maintained to demanding PGA standards year-round.

Featuring 90 holes of golf, the PGA Sheraton Resort offers a variety of challenges at every tee. Four of the courses — the Haig, Squire, General, and Champion — are within steps of the hotel. The fifth and newest, the Estate, is located a short ride away. George and Tom Fazio designed the Champion, Haig, and Squire courses. The General was designed by — and named for — golf legend Arnold Palmer. Karl Litten was the architect of the Estate.

For long-ball hitters the most challenging is the 7,002-yard par-

72 Champion Course. Recently redesigned by Jack Nicklaus, it is the only course in the country remodeled to the specifics of the game of

the Senior PGA Tour Player. It is the permanent home of PGA Seniors' Championship. The Champion sports a Scottish motif, with

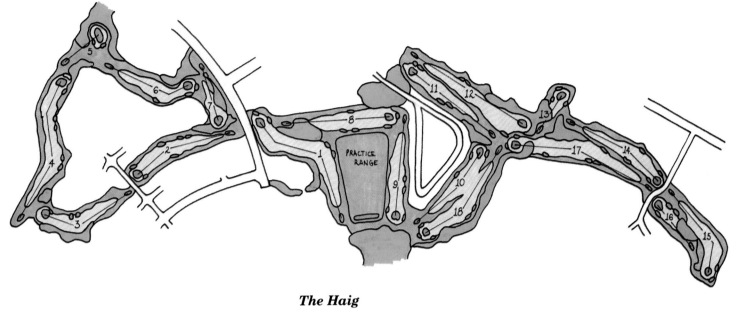

The Haig

Hole	1	2	3	4	5	6	7	8	9	10	11	12	13	14	15	16	17	18
Yards	501	381	392	566	151	393	209	413	387	384	395	513	159	403	361	210	532	456
Par	5	4	4	5	3	4	3	4	4	4	4	5	3	4	4	3	5	4

Yardage: 6,806; Par: 72

mounds and contoured fairways and hazards that come in the form of 107 bunkers and water on 17 holes.

The oldest of the four courses is the Haig, named after the legendary Walter Hagen and opened in March 1980. At 6,806 yards, the course is long, tight and full of trees, which provide a challenge for both low- and high-handicappers to shoot par 72.

The 6,768-yard, par-72 General is a typical links course. With its long, open rolling fairways the wind definitely is a factor.

Short hitters off the tee should consider the Squire, described by George Fazio as a "thinking man's course," because it demands accuracy not distance. Measuring 6,478 yards, the Squire plays to a par 72.

Located about 6 miles west of the resort, the 6,784-yard, par-72 Estate course has TiffDwarf grass on its greens and features open meadows banded by Florida pines, subtropical foliage and many lakes.

For warming up, the resort's practice areas include two driving ranges and three practice greens.

There are 335 rooms, each with a king or two double beds, each with a private terrace or balcony overlooking lake, pool, golf course and panorama of all. In addition, there are 24 one- and two-bedroom suites and two-bedroom, two-bath Cottage Suites that feature fully equipped kitchens.

Recreation amenities include 19 clay tennis courts, a 26-acre sailing lake and a complete health and fitness center, which includes six racquetball courts.

Address: 400 Avenue Of The Champions, Palm Beach Gardens, Fla. 33418
Phone: (407) 627-2000, (800) 325-3535
No. of rooms: 335
No. of holes: 90
Sports facilities: tennis, sailing, pools, health and fitness center
Restaurants: 5
Business facilities: 26,000 square feet of meeting space
Location: 20 miles north of Palm Beach
Nearby attractions: Worth Avenue Shopping-Palm Beach, Burt Reynolds Dinner Theater, jai alai and polo

Miami Lakes Inn
Miami Lakes

Miami Lakes is a 3,000-acre resort community located 18 miles northwest of downtown Miami. Its most celebrated resident is a self-confessed marginal golfer and coach of the NFL's Miami Dolphins, Don Shula.

The secluded and lushly landscaped 25-year-old community is bursting with tropical foliage at every turn, and it has won numerous architectural and design awards.

The community is self-contained with many shops, restaurants and outdoor cafes on Main Street, which serves as the town center.

Guests stay in Mediterranean-style two- and three-story buildings at either the 208-room Miami Lakes Inn or the 102-room Golf Resort. The Inn's 31 suites include built-in wet bars and entertainment areas.

The 7,055-yard, par-72 golf course was built in 1962 and designed by Miami-based architect Bill Watts. It has some of the highest elevated tees in South Florida and large undulating greens. In addition, the golf complex includes a lighted par-3 course and a lighted driving range.

Other amenities include nine tennis courts, two pools, racquetball and a health club.

Miami Lakes

Hole	Yards	Par
1	439	4
2	419	4
3	188	3
4	441	4
5	522	5
6	429	4
7	142	3
8	382	4
9	559	5
10	397	4
11	423	4
12	527	5
13	211	3
14	447	4
15	349	4
16	532	5
17	185	3
18	463	4
7,055		**72**

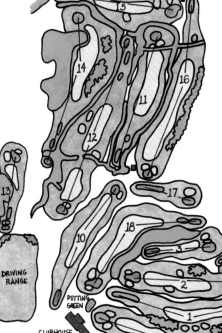

Address: 15255 Bullrun Road, Miami Lakes, Fla. 33014
Phone: (305) 821-1150, (800) 24-LAKES, in Florida (800) 231-4173
No. of rooms: 310
No. of holes: 18
Sports facilities: tennis, racquetball, health club
Restaurants: 4
Business facilities: 15,000 square feet of meeting space with 22 meeting rooms and a tiered lecture hall
Location: 18 miles northwest of Miami
Nearby attractions: Joe Robbie Stadium, Vizcaya, Miami Metrozoo

Cheeca Lodge
Islamorada

Along with President George Bush, celebrities such as Jack Nicklaus, Ted Williams and Paul Newman have been guests at the Cheeca Lodge, located off U.S. Highway 1 at mile marker 82 in Islamorada (Florida Keys), 75 miles south of Miami.

The lodge's nine-hole executive golf course, in fact, was designed by Golforce Inc., the company that builds all of Nicklaus' courses.

The course is ideal for a novice golfer or a serious linkster, offering just enough challenge to keep iron play sharp.

Played twice, the par-3 layout measures 1,658 yards. Offering breathtaking ocean views, the course has strategically placed traps and water hazards. The longest hole is 115 yards, so you may as well leave your woods at home.

Overlooking a 1,000-foot beach, the newly renovated 203-room Cheeca Lodge was built in the 1940s by Clara Mae Downey, owner of the famous Olney Inn in Maryland. In the 1950s, A & P grocery store heirs Carl and Cynthia Twitchell bought the resort, renamed it after Cynthia's nickname and maintained it as a private club.

In the '70s, Cheeca Lodge was purchased by Coca-Cola bottler Carl Navare, an avid fly fisherman and international sportsman. Today, the Navarre family is a limited partner to Cheeca's present owner, the Chicago-based Coastal Hotel Group.

Guest rooms and suites at Cheeca overlook the ocean, lake, golf course and tennis courts. The resort's furniture, custom-made in a British Colonial style, includes teak-stained nightstands and dressers, and bamboo and wicker headboards and chairs.

Golfing fishermen who want to squeeze in a couple of rounds between deep-sea fishing will find the lodge to their liking. Dozens of charter boats head out daily from Islamorada in quest of big-game fish such as cobia, dolphin, blackfin, tuna and marlin. Islamorada bills itself as "the sportfishing capital of the world."

Not to be missed is Cheeca's Atlantic Edge restaurant, which has romantic ocean views and a menu brimming with delights such as stone crab pie, conch chowder and freshly caught Islamorada seafood.

Cheeca Lodge

Hole	Yards	Par
1	83	3
2	80	3
3	89	3
4	98	3
5	81	3
6	107	3
7	72	3
8	90	3
9	104	3
10	102	3
11	89	3
12	97	3
13	88	3
14	99	3
15	96	3
16	93	3
17	75	3
18	115	3
	1,658	**54**

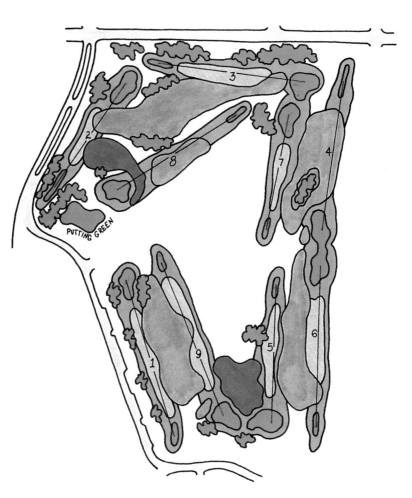

Address: P.O. Box 527, Islamorada, Fla. 33036
Phone: (305) 664-4651, (800) 327-2888
No. of rooms: 203
No. of holes: 9
Sports facilities: tennis, hot tubs, pool, fishing pier
Restaurants: 2
Business facilities: 4,200 square feet, including ocean-front board room and presidential suite
Location: 75 miles south of Miami
Nearby attractions: John Pennekamp Coral Reef State Park, Key West, Theater of the Sea

Doral Resort and Country Club
Miami

The "Blue Monster" is neither a new movie nor a theme-park ride: It's one of Florida's more famous golf courses. The 6,939-yard layout at the Doral Resort and Country Club, west of Miami, is considered one of the nation's toughest.

The course, designed by Dick Wilson, is the site of the PGA Doral-Ryder Open, held in March. A favorite hole for golfers of any skill level is the 246-yard, par-3 13th hole, where even a fairway wood might not be enough club to get you to the green if the wind is kicking up. The 18th hole consistently has been rated the most difficult finishing hole on the PGA Tour. Tour pro Raymond Floyd called it the hardest par 4 in the world. With water on the left side from tee to green and a prevailing wind blowing across the fairway, you better hit your best drive of the day and an equally superb long iron shot or you'll be muttering to yourself all the way to the club-

house.

The Doral Resort and Country Club is one of the world's largest golf resorts, featuring five championship courses and a par-3 executive course. The size of the golf area is overwhelming — 18 miles of fairways, more than 100 acres of lakes and more than 450 sand traps.

With more than 400 golf carts, the resort has one of the largest fleets in the world. Doral's clubhouse contains a three-story, 10,000-square-foot pro shop, the largest in Florida.

After you get through with the "Blue Monster," or, in some cases, after it gets through with you, the other courses include: the Red (6,180 yards), designed by Wilson and Bob von Hagge; the Gold (6,444 yards) and Silver (6,801 yards), designed by von Hagge and Bruce Devlin; and the White (6,208 yards), designed by von Hagge.

If your swing needs work, you're in the right place. The Ballard School, featuring teaching pro Jimmy Ballard, offers a variety of instructional packages with accommodations at Doral.

Doral has 650 rooms and suites in eight three- and four-story

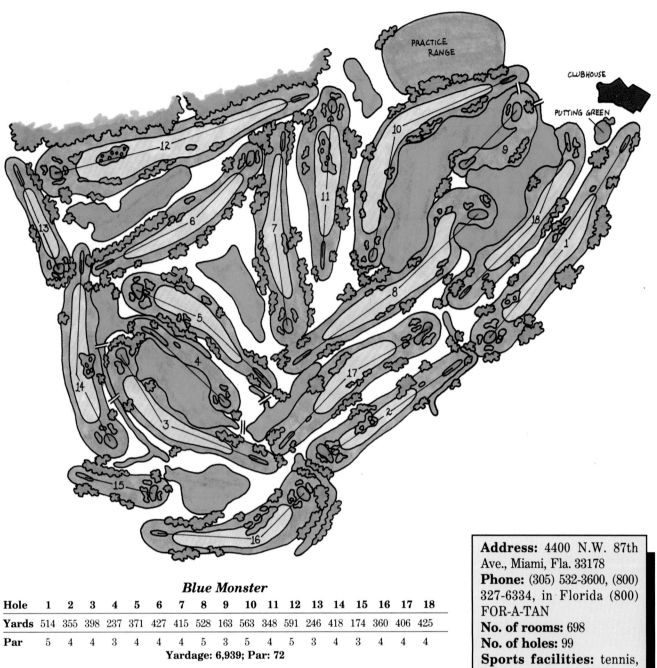

Blue Monster

Hole	1	2	3	4	5	6	7	8	9	10	11	12	13	14	15	16	17	18
Yards	514	355	398	237	371	427	415	528	163	563	348	591	246	418	174	360	406	425
Par	5	4	4	3	4	4	4	5	3	5	4	5	3	4	3	4	4	4

Yardage: 6,939; Par: 72

lodges, central to the clubhouse and in close proximity to the resort's Olympic-size pool. All of the resort's rooms and suites have been renovated and include a private terrace, mirrored dressing room, oversized bath, refrigerator and mini bar.

Aches and pains acquired from too many rounds of golf can be soothed at Doral's Saturnia International Spa, a plush European-inspired facility where health-related activities like herbal wraps, mineral salt soaks, saunas and Swiss showers are the order of the day. The spa features 48 luxury suites, all with expansive views of rolling hills and lush gardens.

There are 15 all-weather tennis courts within the 2,400-acre complex as well as a bicycle and jogging path that winds around the golf courses, a 24-stable equestrian center, and some excellent bass fishing in the well-stocked golf course lakes.

Address: 4400 N.W. 87th Ave., Miami, Fla. 33178
Phone: (305) 532-3600, (800) 327-6334, in Florida (800) FOR-A-TAN
No. of rooms: 698
No. of holes: 99
Sports facilities: tennis, bicycling, pool, spa and exercise facility
Restaurants: 6
Business facilities: More than 75,000 square feet of meeting space, including the Grand Ballroom that can accommodate up to 1,200 people
Location: Miami area
Nearby attractions: Miami Art Deco Historical District, Bayside Marketplace, Vizcaya Museum and Gardens, Lowe Art Museum

Best Of The Rest

As one of the world's most dynamic golf areas, Southeast Florida has several other fine resorts that feature golf as an amenity.

The Rolling Hills Golf Resort in Fort Lauderdale, which served as the location for the movie *Caddy Shack*, has 27 holes of golf with majestic Spanish Oaks lining many of the fairways.

Another Fort Lauderdale resort that is golf-friendly is the Inverrary, which has two 18-hole golf courses and an 18-hole, par-60 course.

In Miami, the 131-acre Kings Bay Resort sports a challenging 6,556-yard, par-72 layout designed by Mark Mahannah.

In the Florida Keys near Marathon, the Hawk's Cay Resort & Marina, situated on a 60-acre island, is the ideal spot for fishing enthusiasts and golfers.

Rolling Hills Golf Resort
3501 West Rolling Hills
Fort Lauderdale, Fla. 33328
(305) 475-0400, (800) 327-7735
27 holes

Inverrary, A Club & Resort
3501 Inverrary Blvd.
Fort Lauderdale, Fla. 33319
(305) 485-0500
54 holes

Kings Bay Resort
14401 SW 62nd Ave.
Miami, Fla. 33158
(305) 235-7161
18 holes

Hawk's Cay Resort & Marina
Mile Marker 61
Marathon, Fla. 33050
(305) 743-7000, (800) 327-7775
18 holes

Other Courses To Consider

Arrowhead Country Club
(semiprivate)
8201 SW 24th St.
Fort Lauderdale, Fla. 33324
(305) 475-8200
18 holes

Atlantis Country Club
(semiprivate)
190 Atlantis Blvd.
Lake Worth, Fla. 33462
(407) 965-7700
18 holes

Biltmore Golf Course (public)
1210 Anastasia
Coral Gables, Fla. 33134
(305) 442-6485
18 holes

Costa Del Sol Golf & Racquet Club
(resort)
100 Costa Del Sol Blvd.
Miami, Fla. 33178
(305) 592-9210
18 holes

Biltmore Golf Course

Crystal Lake Country Club
(semiprivate)
3800 Crystal Lake Drive
Pompano, Fla. 33060
(305) 943-3700
18 holes

Del Ray Beach Country Club
(public)
2200 Highland Ave.
Delray Beach, Fla. 33445
(407) 278-0808
18 holes

Emerald Dunes (public)
2100 E. Dunes Drive
West Palm Beach, Fla. 33411
(407) 684-GOLF
18 holes

Indian River Plantation (resort)
385 N.E. Plantation Road
Hutchinson Island, Fla. 33996
(305) 225-2700, (800) 327-4873
18 holes

Indian River Plantation

Lake Worth Golf Club (public)
1 North Seventh Ave.
Lake Worth, Fla. 33460
(407) 533-7364
18 holes

Lucerne Lakes (public)
144 Lucerne Lakes Blvd.
Lake Worth, Fla. 33467
(407) 967-6810
18 holes

Meadowood (semiprivate)
3001 Johnston Road
Fort Pierce, Fla. 34951
(407) 464-5500
18 holes

Miami Springs Country Club
(public)
650 Curtiss Parkway
Miami Springs, Fla. 33166
(305) 888-2377
18 holes

Key Biscayne Golf Club

Kendale Lakes Golf & Country
Club (semiprivate)
6401 Kendale Lakes Drive
Miami, Fla. 33183
(305) 382-3935
18 holes

Key Biscayne Golf Club (public)
6400 Crandon Blvd.
Miami, Fla. 33149
(305) 361-9129
18 holes

Palm Beach Lakes Golf Club
(public)
1100 Congress Ave.
West Palm Beach, Fla. 33401
(407) 683-2700
18 holes

9

Boca West in Boca Raton

The Florida Golf Lifestyle

It's a safe bet the following scenario has been played out a few thousand times at Florida resorts: A golfer waiting to tee off suddenly loses concentration. He thinks about his wife and kids splashing around in the pool. He feels the soft, warm sea breeze blowing through his hair. He relishes the vibrant color surrounding him — the verdant green of the golf course, the brilliant blue sky. Then he remembers the February snow storm and gray skies awaiting him up North when his golf getaway ends. In his subconscious a whisper advises, "Hey, you're no polar bear. Why don't you just buy a house on a golf course down here?"

Few golfers who have roamed Florida fairways would deny they have dreamed of buying a home, condo or villa on a golf course in the Sunshine State.

Like any real estate purchase, when you consider buying into the Florida golf course community lifestyle, the questions multiply quick-er than the shots on one of those monstrous-bunkered par 5s.

In general, there are four types of planned communities:

■ **Resort/residential:** Hotels and villas are surrounded by multiple golf courses and a lot of tennis, boating, water sports, shopping, dining and entertainment. Some resort developments use security gates to separate residential areas from resort traffic.

■ **Semiprivate residential:** The community is private, often with security gates and separate living villages. The golf course or courses, however, are open to the public. Occasionally, after enough members are secured, the course will close play to the public.

■ **Private residential:** Only members and their guests are allowed to play on the golf course. Strict guidelines determine the use and maintenance of the course. Home buyers generally pay a premium for seclusion and security as well as upscale amenities.

■ **Equity club:** Property owners have an opportunity to buy equity in the ownership of the golf course, clubhouse and other common properties. Equity clubs almost always are private communities, although some offer temporary outside membership during the early stages of development.

Most golfers on a Florida vacation are more likely to be exposed to the resort/residential community because that's where most of the golf package stays are available. Real estate experts caution golfers not to be swayed by their emotions. The "golf vacation of a lifetime" may not be the buy of a lifetime.

"People should not be impulsive," says Dick Lumsden, marketing consultant for Bluewater Bay, a 1,800-acre resort and residential community located near Niceville in Northwest Florida. "They should analyze a resort beyond its amenities. After all, most of their time will not be spent on the golf course or on the tennis courts. It's a good idea to ask questions about the community, such as how many part-time residents there are, how many full-time, and how many are involved in the rental program. Also, visit the resort more than once so you can get a better idea of what it would be like living at or visiting a community once you decide to buy."

Lumsden concedes that one of the main reasons people buy at resorts is the amenities.

Chuck Holt agrees. He is vice president of sales for Grenelefe Realty Inc., which handles sales for Grenelefe Resort near Haines City in Central Florida. "The golf courses at most resorts are always in excellent condition because of the intense competition that exists between resorts. Also, there is a kind of one-upmanship that exists between resorts when it comes to recreational amenities. For instance, at our tennis facility we just added two grass courts," Holt said. "You just don't find many golf-oriented residential communities with the recreational amenities an upscale resort offers."

Holt adds that many resort residents enjoy the steady influx of vacationers that brings in new people to meet, but other residents do not.

"They should ask themselves that question when they are making the decision to buy or not to buy," he said. "They may also not like the fact they have to share the amenities."

Holt said many resorts have devised rewards for residents, who have proven to be the best sources for word-of-mouth advertising, especially on the golf course when they're teamed up with guests.

For instance, residents at Gren-

elefe receive a VIP logo pin that entitles them to special attention, like preferred seating in the resort's restaurants. Residents also receive discounts on food and merchandise (20 percent in-season and 10 percent off-season) as well as guaranteed tee times (37 percent of tee times are reserved for owners) on the resort's three championship courses.

At Innisbrook, a sprawling resort layout with 63 holes of golf north of Tampa in Tarpon Springs, residents receive a 25 percent discount on food and beverages year-round.

Yet, for all the inherent amenities and advantages that make day-to-day living a breeze, resorts attract many buyers seeking an investment rather than a permanent residence. Owners can help offset mortgage payments by renting their units to vacationers.

"People need to know that it's not a get-rich-quick situation," cautions Dominic A. Benjivengo, president of Golf Host Securities Inc., brokers for Innisbrook. "Still, in the long run it does allow an owner to vacation at a cost significantly less than [if he were] a hotel guest."

There are two types of rental programs — rental pool and rental management. Here is how they work:

■ **Rental pool:** Owners who place their unit in a pool receive income regardless of occupancy. For example, at Innisbrook 53 percent of gross room revenue goes into the rental pool. Of that number, 80 percent is for common distribution. Owners receive a settlement based upon the number of days their apartment was available for rental and the size of the unit.

■ **Rental management:**

Owners receive a settlement only if their specific unit is rented. A management fee, which differs from resort to resort, is subtracted, and the owner receives the remaining sum.

Finding the right resort development is as easy as spending a vacation at the resort and analyzing its golf courses, facilities and real estate options. Florida resort-residential communities offer a combination of single-family homes, villas, condos, townhomes or patio homes as well as home sites.

The Sunshine State has dozens of options to appease even the most discerning potential resort resident. In Northwest Florida, resort communities such as Bay Point in Panama City and Sandestin in Destin offer golf- and water-oriented lifestyles. Near Jacksonville, Amelia Island Plantation features an island lifestyle, and Sawgrass spans 4,800 acres with access to five championship golf courses. Farther south, Saddlebrook in Wesley Chapel near Tampa attracts buyers with two Arnold Palmer-designed layouts, and Palm Beach Polo & Country Club in West Palm Beach is known for its 45 holes of golf and multimillion-dollar equestrian center.

"The great thing about buying into an established resort is that you're not buying something that's on a drawing board, where promises often don't become realities," says Grenelefe's Holt, a 25-year veteran in real estate. "At established resorts, potential residents can see the course or courses they'll play on and other facilities they can enjoy. They are better able to envision the type of life they can have, whether visiting or living there day to day."

Holt points out that buying into a resort is one of the best ways for buyers to get luxury for less. "Think about it," he says. "Where can you get all these amenities without care and maintenance worries?"

Holt best sums up the appeal of buying at a Florida resort when he says, "People just love the fact that they live at a place where other people pay to vacation. A resort resident has a certain amount of pride because of that."

Florida, which has 1,000 golf courses, is the forerunner in multi-amenity, golf course-oriented communities. According to the National Golf Foundation, 80 percent of the courses in Florida either on the drawing board or under construction in 1989 were connected to real estate developments. Before 1986, less than 10 percent of all new courses were real estate-related.

With such a dynamic market, there are hundreds of communities from which to select. Many experts agree that the trend in the 1990s in Florida is toward master-planned communities: residential developments where residents can engage in many of life's daily activities of working, playing, shopping and going to school. These communities have uniform housing styles, shopping and commerce areas, and recreational facilities.

Some of the Sunshine State's high-profile, master-planned communities include Sawgrass in Ponte Vedra Beach; Palm Coast, near Daytona Beach; Tampa Palms Golf & Country Club; Lake Nona and MetroWest in Orlando; Gateway in Fort Myers; PGA National in Palm Beach Gardens; St. Lucie West in Port St. Lucie; and Pelican Bay in Naples.

Heathrow, off Interstate 4 north

Lake Nona in Orlando

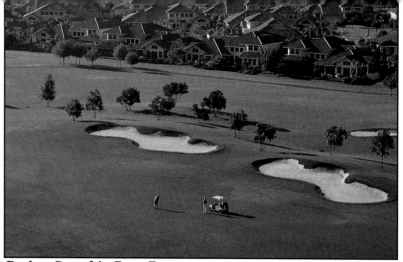
Broken Sound in Boca Raton

of Orlando, is a prime example of the master-planned golf community concept. The brainchild of Jeno Paulucci, the 3,300-acre upscale, self-contained development surrounding a Ron Garl-designed golf course is striving to be a city within a city. In place are single-family homes, townhomes, villas, an apartment complex, international business center and shopping complex. Heathrow also is home to the national headquarters of the American Automobile Association.

"Golfers and non-golfers living in places like Heathrow can enjoy life to its fullest because they don't waste time leaving the community to fulfill all their needs, leaving more time for golf and recreation," says Roger Hall, chairman and chief executive officer of the Arvida Co., which is developing the residential side of Heathrow.

The Boca Raton-based development firm has been an innovator in the golf course community lifestyle for more than 30 years. Many of the features that are staples at upscale golf course real estate developments, such as landscaping, golf courses designed by top-name architects, security, and architectural control, were introduced by Arvida more than 15 years ago.

What can Florida golf course real estate buyers expect in the communities being developed in the 1990s?

Says Hall: "Time and time again property values in Florida golf communities have increased. With the soaring popularity of golf, I see that trend continuing.

"An important aspect of communities in the 1990s will be the development of appealing amenities that complement the golf course. I think passive park areas and open spaces, where families can enjoy themselves, will be increasingly popular. Security will continue to be an amenity desired by many homeowners."

Hall predicts that the Baby Boom generation will have a profound impact on determining what will be popular in the next decade as they move full force into the market.

"Some of the trendiest amenities in the 1990s, I believe, will be culturally related," Hall said. "For example, at Weston, one of our master-planned communities near Fort Lauderdale, we have a bandshell where concerts, plays and other events are staged regularly. And there is a community [Pelican Bay] in Naples that has a performing arts facility on property. Without a doubt, we'll see more and more of this type of amenity in the future."

Amenities are just one of hundreds of considerations prospective buyers must evaluate before they purchase. Among the others are history of the community; location; access from your present home; climate; quality of cultural, recreational and economic opportunities in the region; and type of community.

All of these factors and numerous others need to be studied carefully, and for a serious golfer, the golf course evaluation should be high on the list. After all, if you end up despising the golf course you'll play on more than any other, how enjoyable can your recreational life be?

Once you start looking at development courses, you'll have more than a few questions. How does the course play? Is it designed for a pro or a hacker? Is it engulfed by so many condos and villas that they're as much a hazard as the bunkers and lakes? Is it a quality course that will enhance property values? Does it matter who designed it?

When evaluating a golf course at a development, go beyond the "playability" question if you want to make a purchase you'll be happy with years down the road.

Carefully consider the designer of the course. The course designer can help increase property values, create prestige and contribute greatly to the development's image.

Arnold Palmer and Jack Nicklaus might be considered the Ralph Lauren and Pierre Cardin of golf course designers, but they are by no means the only designers with marquee value. Course architects who have established name identification nationally, and especially in Florida, include Lloyd Clifton, Pete Dye, Tom Fazio, Ron Garl, Arthur Hills, Robert Trent Jones, Joe Lee, Mark McCumber and Ed Seay.

Clearly, the styles of the various designers differ. But the consistent factor is that once the course is completed, the designer's name always is mentioned in the same breath with the development. Very few times do you see a golf course development advertisement where the designer's name is not included, providing it is a recognizable name.

The marketing concept of using names to help sell developments took hold in the early 1960s in Florida, when entertainers such as George Gobel and Steve Allen and baseball superstar Ted Williams began promoting housing developments. At the time, Florida was saddled with a reputation for shady land deals, and developers were attempting to establish credibility. Today, as the golfing public has become more educated to course design techniques, a noted designer can provide instant credibility. If the course is outstanding, the development reaps additional benefits of recognition and increases its chance of being successful.

So, how do you evaluate a development course when you've been attracted by a big-name designer? Here are some things to consider:

■ Judge the course carefully as you would any major purchase. Is the course a series of flashy design gimmicks to attract attention? Is the layout designed in a style you like? (Scottish? Traditional? Modern traditional? Gimmicky?)

■ Study the track record of the designer thoroughly. What other courses has he designed? How long has he been designing courses?

■ Research the particular styles of designers. For instance, Nicklaus is known for special effects using mounds, swales and hollows to create depth, which gives the course instant maturity. Jones prefers designs with strategically placed bunkers from tee to green. Fazio has a penchant for placing no cross hazards in fairways. Dye is noted for the railroad-tie look around tiered greens. And

Garl is a master at using the existing natural elements to highlight a course.

■ Determine the designer's involvement. Does he have an investment? Was he a consultant or a designer? Will he reside at the development? These and other questions can help determine the long-range prospects of the development. Clearly, if the designer is bullish on the development, that is a good sign.

■ Find out at what stage of development the course was planned. Most developers demand the right to plan the community first and allow the owner to place the golf course on whatever land is remaining. Sometimes the greatest designer has trouble taking a small piece of land and turning it into a great course. The ideal is when the course assumes as much importance as the housing.

■ Find out how much emphasis will be given to golf with regard to the entire recreational lineup.

■ Finally, evaluate golf amenities such as the clubhouse, driving range, practice putting green, parking, etc.

Suffice it to say, you'll have more questions about the course and an almost inexhaustible number of real estate questions. If you do your homework, you're more likely to be satisfied with your investment, not to mention rounds and rounds of enjoyment on a course you love to play.

The Florida golf real estate market is ever-changing with options. The offerings run the gamut from golf courses in developments featuring recreational vehicle sites to manufactured housing, amenity-rich resorts with hotels and villas, typical suburban neighborhoods with single-family homes, ultra-ex-

clusive private communities, self-contained master-planned communities, and dozens of variations. Whether you're looking for a permanent home, retirement home, second home or investment property on or near a golf course, Florida's market has something for every golfer's skill level and budget.

Buyers in the Florida market should expect to pay a premium of 15 percent to 25 percent for lots with golf course exposure, says Bill Owen, president of Real Estate Research Consultants Inc., an Orlando-based firm whose clients include several major Florida golf course communities.

Whatever your price range, you'll find an outstanding selection of homes, villas, condos and building sites.

In addition to some of the best golf courses in the nation, Florida has other pluses, such as a temperate climate, a lot of water for aesthetic beauty and recreational purposes, sports activities, attractions, entertainment options and cultural offerings.

Besides the enviable aspects of a tropical Florida lifestyle, buying into a golf course community in the state comes with other advantages. Studies show that a golf course provides a sense of community as well as increasing lot and home values.

If after playing at one of Florida's golf resorts the idea of living on the links has you hooked, take heart. You've taken the first step toward understanding the wonders of the Florida golf lifestyle. Now, with some homework and a lot of planning you may end up taking a permanent golf vacation where those visions of snowy days and gray skies no longer will destroy your concentration on the tee.

10

Your Florida Golf Source

Without a doubt, planning is the secret to a successful Florida golf getaway. A few phone calls and several letters will garner most golfers more information than they'll need. Here are some addresses and lists to help you compile the facts and figures you'll need to make an educated decision.

Tourism information

Florida has one of the world's more developed tourism infrastructures, and tourism offices throughout the state welcome visitors' requests for information about destinations and actitivies in their particular region. Be sure and mention specific activities and areas you're interested in.

Florida Division of Tourism
Visitor Inquiry Section
107 W. Gaines St.
Fletcher Building, Room 422
Tallahassee, Fla. 32399-2000
(904) 487-1462

NORTHWEST:
Panama City Visitors and Convention Bureau
P.O. Box 9473
Panama City Beach, Fla. 32407
(800) 327-8352

Pensacola Visitors and Convention Bureau
1401 E. Gregory St.
Pensacola, Fla. 32501
(904) 434-1234, (800) 343-4321

Tallahassee Convention & Visitors Bureau
100 N. Duval St.
Tallahassee, Fla. 32302
(904) 681-9200

NORTHEAST:
Jacksonville Convention and Visitors Bureau
33 Hogan St., Suite 250
Jacksonville, Fla. 32202
(904) 353-9736

St. Augustine & St. Johns County Chamber of Commerce
52 Castillo Drive
St. Augustine, Fla. 32085
(904) 829-5681

CENTRAL:
Destination Daytona
126 E. Orange Ave.
Daytona Beach, Fla. 32114
(904) 255-0415, (800) 854-1234

Kissimmee-St. Cloud Convention and Visitors Bureau
P.O. Box 422007
Kissimmee, Fla. 34742-2007
(407) 847-5000, in Florida (800) 432-9199, (800) 327-9159

Ocala-Marion County Chamber of Commerce
P.O. Box 1210
Ocala, Fla. 32678
(904) 629-8051

Orlando/Orange County Convention and Visitors Bureau
7208 Sand Lake Road, Suite 300
Orlando, Fla. 32819
(407) 363-5800

UPPER WEST COAST:
Pinellas Suncoast Tourist Development Council
4625 E. Bay Drive, Suite 109A
Clearwater, Fla. 34620
(813) 530-6452

Tampa/Hillsborough Convention and Visitors Association Inc.
111 Madison St., Suite 1010
Tampa, Fla. 33602-4706
(800) 826-8358, (813) 223-1111

SOUTHWEST:
Lee County Tourist Development Council
P.O. Box 2445
Fort Myers, Fla. 33902
(800) 237-6444

Manatee Convention and Visitors Bureau
P.O. Box 788
Bradenton, Fla. 34206-0788
(813) 746-5989

Naples Area Chamber of Commerce
1700 N. Ninth Street
Naples, Fla. 33940
(813) 262-6141

Sanibel-Captiva Island Chamber of Commerce
P.O. Box 166
Sanibel Island, Fla. 33957
(813) 472-3232

Sarasota County Chamber of Commerce
P.O. Box 308
Sarasota, Fla. 34230
(813) 955-8187

SOUTHEAST:
Greater Fort Lauderdale Convention and Visitors Bureau
500 E. Broward Blvd., Suite 104
Fort Lauderdale, Fla. 33394
(305) 765-4466, (800) 356-1662

Greater Miami Convention and Visitors Bureau
701 Brickell Ave., Suite 2700
Miami, Fla. 33131
(800) 641-1111

Monroe County Tourist Development Council
P.O. Box 866
Key West, Fla. 33041
(305) 296-2228

Palm Beach County Convention and Visitors Bureau
1555 Palm Beach Lakes Blvd., Suite 204
West Palm Beach, Fla. 33401
(407) 471-3995

Golf packaging companies

Golfpac Inc.
P.O. Box 940490
Maitland, Fla. 32794-0490
(800) 327-0878, (407) 660-8277

Regal Retreats
2039 North Meridian, Suite 145
Tallahassee, Fla. 32303
(904) 386-2277

World of Golf
231 Semoran Commerce Place
Apopka, Fla. 32703
(800) 729-1400, (407) 884-8300

Discount cards

American Lung Association Golf Privilege Card
(407) 898-3401, (800) 624-8735

Fellowship of Christian Athletes Golf Card
P.O. Box 45103
Sarasota, Fla. 34277-4103
(813) 371-5954, (813) 954-0848

The Golf Card
1137 E. 2100 South
Salt Lake City, Utah 84152-6439
(800) 453-4260, in Canada (800) 321-8269

The Golfweek VIP Card
P.O. Box 1458
Winter Haven, Fla. 33882
(813) 294-5511

The Greens Card
P.O. Box 10485
Naples, Fla. 33941-9955
(813) 643-4616

North Florida PGA Passport
P.O. Box 561045
Orlando, Fla. 32856
(407) 894-4653

United States Golf Card Association Inc.
P.O. Box 5493
Indian Rocks Beach, Fla. 34635
(813) 972-9337

Major golf organizations

Ladies Professional Golf Association (LPGA)
2570 Volusia Ave., Suite B
Daytona Beach, Fla. 32114
(904) 254-8800

National Golf Foundation
1150 S. U.S. Highway 1
Jupiter, Fla. 33477
(407) 744-6006

PGA Tour
Sawgrass
112 TPC Blvd.
Ponte Vedra, Fla. 32082
(904) 285-3700

Professional Golfers Association of America
100 Avenue of the Champions
Palm Beach Gardens, Fla. 33418
(407) 624-8400

Florida Tour events

Oldsmobile LPGA Classic
Wycliffe Golf & Country Club
Lake Worth

Royal Caribbean Classic (Senior PGA)
Key Biscayne Golf Club
Key Biscayne

GTE Suncoast Classic (Senior PGA)
Tampa Palms Country Club
Tampa

Aetna Challenge (Senior PGA)
THE CLUB at Pelican Bay
Naples

Phar-Mor Inverrary Classic (LPGA)
Inverrary Golf Club
Lauderhill

Chrysler Cup (Senior PGA)
TPC Prestancia
Sarasota

Doral Ryder Open (PGA)
Doral Resort & Country Club
Miami

Honda Classic (PGA)
TPC at Eagle Trace
Coral Springs

The Players Championship (PGA)
TPC at Sawgrass
Ponte Vedra

Panama City Beach Classic (Ben Hogan)
Hombre Golf Club
Panama City Beach

The Nestle Invitational (PGA)
Bay Hill Country Club
Orlando

Lake City Classic (Ben Hogan)
Lake City Country Club
Lake City

PGA Seniors Championship (Senior PGA)
PGA National Golf Club
Palm Beach Gardens

Pensacola Open (Ben Hogan)
Pensacola Country Club
Pensacola

Gateway Open (Ben Hogan)
Gateway Golf Club
Fort Myers

Fairfield Barnett Space Coast
Classic (Senior PGA)
Suntree Country Club
Melbourne

Centel Classic (LPGA)
Site to be announced
Tallahassee

Walt Disney World Classic (PGA)
Magnolia, Palm and Lake Buena
Vista Golf Courses
Lake Buena Vista

JC Penney Classic (PGA/LPGA)
Innisbrook Resort
Tarpon Springs

Team Championship (PGA)
Palm Beach Polo & Country Club
West Palm Beach

Golf publications

Florida Golfer
201 S. Airport Road
Naples, Fla. 33942
(813) 643-4994

Golf Coast Magazine
P.O. Box 20578
St. Petersburg, Fla. 33742
(813) 522-4147

Golfweek Newspaper
P.O. Box 1458
Winter Haven, Fla. 33882
(813) 294-5511

Senior Golfer
1323 S.E. 17th St.
Suite 179
Fort Lauderdale, Fla. 33316
(305) 527-0778

Tee Times Magazine
P.O. Box 561045
Orlando, Fla. 32856
(407) 422-4653

Golf hot lines

(900) 990-4653 (cost $1.95 first minute, 95 cents each additional minute). Sponsored by Golfweek Publications, offers information on Florida golf course real estate, public and private golf courses, tournaments and special golf packages. (800) 666-4482 — Golf Illustrated's Travel Center — travel information and bookings.

Golf instruction

Ben Sutton Golf School
Sun City Center (near Tampa)
Mailing Adress: Box 9199, Canton, Ohio 44711
(216) 453-4350

Doral Resort and Country Club
Jimmy Ballard Golf Workshop
4400 N.W. 87th Ave.
Miami, Fla. 33178-2192
(305) 592-2000

Grenelefe Resort & Conference
Center
Howie Barrow Golf School
3200 State Road 546
Grenelefe, Fla. 33844-9732
(813) 422-7511

Hyatt Regency Grand Cypress
Jack Nicklaus Golf Academy
1 N. Jacaranda
Orlando, Fla. 32819
(407) 239-1975, (800) 835-7377

Innisbrook Resort
Innisbrook Golf Institute
P.O. Drawer 1088
Tarpon Springs, Fla. 34688-1088
(813) 942-2000

Miami Lakes Inn and Resort
Bill Skelley Schools of Golf
15255 Bull Run Road
Miami Lakes, Fla. 33014
(800) 231-4173

Mission Inn Golf and Tennis
Resort
Mission Inn Golf School
10400 County Road 48
Howey-in-the-Hills, Fla. 34737
(904) 324-3101, (800) 874-9053, in
Florida (800) 342-4495

Plantation Inn and Golf Resort
The Golf School at Mount Snow
(winter home)
P.O. Box 1116
Crystal River, Fla. 32629
(904) 795-4211

Sebring Golf School
4800 Haw Branch Road
Sebring, Fla. 33872
(800) 673-7686

Sheraton Bonaventure Resort and
Spa
John Jacobs' Practical Golf School
Mailing address: 7350 East Evans
Drive, Suite C112, Scottsdale, Ariz.
85260
(602) 991-8587, (800) 472-5007

Vince Cali Golf Schools
925 Appleton Ave.
Orlando, Fla. 32806
(407) 857-4653

Walt Disney World Resort
Walt Disney World Golf Studio
P.O. Box 10000
Lake Buena Vista, Fla. 32830
(407) 824-2288

The index

A

Aetna Challenge 91, 141
Airco Golf Club 89
Allen, Steve 139
Amelia Island Plantation 18, 20, 44, 45, 136
American Automobile Association 138
American Lung Association Golf Privilege Card 19, 141
Amick, Bill 13, 21, 28, 30, 41, 48
Armour, Tommy 114
Arrowhead Country Club 133
Arvida Company 138
Atlantis Country Club 133

B

Babe Zaharias Golf Club 89
Baker-Finch, Ian 74
Ballard Golf School, The 131, 142
Ballard, Jimmy 131
Bardmoor Country Club 89
Bay Hill 19, 75, 80
Bay Hill Classic 57
Bayou Golf Club 89
Bean, Andy 63, 91
Bellair Country Club 84
Belleview Biltmore Resort Hotel 84, 85
Ben Sutton Golf School 142
Benjivengo, Dominic 136
Bill Skelly Schools of Golf 142
Biltmore Golf Course 133
Black Diamond Ranch 19, 22
Bloomingdale Golfers Club 89
Bluewater Bay 20, 27, 36, 37, 135
Bobby Jones Golf Club 106
Boca Raton Resort and Club 114, 115
Breakers, The 110, 111
Buffalo Creek 106
Burnt Store Marina Resort 96
Bush, George 19, 128
Byrd, Willard 35, 111

C

Cahall, Randy 22, 24, 25
Cardin, Pierre 138
Celano, Paul 24, 73
Centel Classic 142
Chadwick, Clarence 94
Cheeca Lodge 128
Chrysler Cup 91, 141
Citrus Hills Golf & Country Club 89
Clarke, C.C. 60
Clifton, Lloyd 13, 60, 66, 138
Coastal Hotel Group 128
Comfort Inn on Perdido Key 30
Coral Oaks Golf Club 106
Costa Del Sol Golf & Racquet Club 133
Crystal Lake Country Club 134

D

Davis, Jr., Sammy 122
Del Ray Beach Country Club 134
DeSoto, Hernando 92
Destination Daytona 140
Devlin, Bruce 34, 106, 131
Diamond, Neil 116
Diplomat Resort and Country Club 122, 123

Disney Inn 65
Doral Resort & Country Club 17, 109, 130, 131, 142
Doral Ryder Open 141
Downey, Clara Mae 128
Dubsdread Golf Course 76
Dunedin Country Club 89
Dunes Golf and Country Club 100
Dye, P.B. 112
Dye, Pete 13, 22, 38, 40, 42, 44, 52, 53, 108, 112, 113, 138, 139

E

Eagle Creek 91
East Bay Country Club 89
Eastwood Country Club 106
Eckerd, Jack 70
Edgewater Beach Resort 17
Eglin Air Force Base Golf Club 38
Embassy Suites 17
Emerald Dunes 134
Errol Country Club 76

F

Fairfield Barnett Space Coast Classic 142
Fawcett, Farrah 121
Fazio, George 111, 120, 124, 125
Fazio, Tom 13, 20, 22, 36, 41, 44, 49, 57, 106, 108, 112, 113, 124, 138, 139
Fellowship of Christian Athletes Golf Card 141
Fiddlesticks 91
Finger, Joe 38
Flagler, Henry 108
Flori-Bama Golf Holiday Package 18
Florida Division of Tourism 140
Florida Golf School 85
Florida Golfer 142
Florida Tour 57
Florida Women's Open 82
Floyd, Raymond 13, 118, 130
Flynn, William 114
Ford, Gerald 114
Fort George Island Golf Club 55
Foxfire Golf Club 106

G

GTE Suncoast Classic 141
Gabor, Zsa Zsa 116
Garl, Ron 13, 20, 21, 46, 62, 63, 71, 75, 89, 91, 96, 102, 106, 108, 112, 113, 138, 139
Gateway Golf Club 106
Gateway Open 142
Gillespie, John Hamilton 91
Glen Abbey Golf Club 76
Gobel, George 139
Golden Gate Golf Club 106
Golden Ocala 20, 75
Golf Card, The 18, 141
Golf Club of Jacksonville 55
Golf Coast Magazine 142
Golf Digest 40
Golf Host Securities 136
Golf Illustrated's Travel Center 142
Golf School at Mount Snow 142
Golf School, The 82
Golf Traveler Magazine 18

Golforce Inc. 128
Golfpac 17, 141
Golfweek 18, 142
Golfweek hot line 142
Golfweek VIP Card 141
Goolagong, Evonne 91
Grand Cypress Resort 13, 20, 57, 58, 73, 74, 142
Great Outdoors, The 70, 71
Greater Fort Lauderdale Convention and Visitors Bureau 141
Greater Miami Convention and Visitors Bureau 141
Greens Card, The 141
Grenelefe Realty Inc. 136
Grenelefe Resort 13, 17, 18, 20, 22, 59, 62, 63, 136, 142
Griffin, Fred 57
Griffin, Merv 121
Groppel, Dr. Jack 80

H

Hagen, Walter 125
Hall, Roger 138
Hammock Dunes 40, 48, 49
Hammond, Donnie 57
Harris, Phil 114
Hawk's Cay Resort 133
Heard, Jerry 95
Heathrow 57, 137, 138
Hills, Arthur 91, 106, 108
Holiday Inn 17
Holt, Chuck 136, 137
Hombre Golf Club 38
Honda Classic 141
Hospitality Inn 30
Howie Barrow Golf School 63, 142
Hunter's Creek Golf Course 76
Hunter's Green Country Club 89
Hyatt Regency 74

I

Indian Bayou Golf & Country Club 38
Indian River Plantation 134
Indigo Lakes Resort 66, 67
Innisbrook Golf Institute 88, 142
Innisbrook Resort 18, 78, 86, 87, 88, 136, 142
International Golf Club 76
Inverness Golf & Country Club 89
Inverrary 133

J

JC Penney Classic 142
Jack Nicklaus Golf Academy 57, 74, 142
Jackson, Tom 33
Jacksonville Beach Golf Club 55
Jacksonville Convention and Visitors Bureau 140
Jacksonville Naval Air Station 55
Jenkins, Dan 40, 41
John Jacobs Golf School 116, 142
Jones, Sr., Robert Trent 40, 42, 57, 62, 75, 114, 118, 138, 139

K

Kendale Lake Golf & Country Club 134
Key Biscayne Golf Club 134
Killearn Country Club & Inn 22, 28, 29
Killearn Estates 29

Kinemation Golf Studio 57
Kings Bay Resort & Marina 133
Kissimmee-St. Cloud Convention and Visitors
    Bureau 140
L
LPGA Qualifying School 66
La Cita Golf & Country Club 75, 76
Ladies Professional Golf Association (LPGA) 58,
    66, 91, 141
Lake City Classic 142
Lake Nona 19, 22, 137
Lake Worth Golf Club 134
Lauren, Ralph 138
Lawrence, Red 122
Leadbetter, David 57
Lee County Tourist Development Council 140
Lee, Joe 13, 40, 42, 64, 68, 69, 111, 114, 116, 138
Lehigh Resort, 104, 105
Links of Lake Bernadette 89
Litten, Karl 124
Longboat Key Club, 92
Lopez, Nancy 91
Lucerne Lakes 134
Ludlum, Robert 91
Lumsden, Dick 135, 136
Lye, Mark 91
M
MacDill Air Force Base Golf Club 89
Magnolia Point 55
Magnolia Valley Golf & Country Club 89
Mahanna, Charlie 116
Mahannah, Mark 82, 133
Majette Dunes Golf & Country Club 38
Manatee Convention and Visitors Bureau 140
Manatee County Golf Club 106
Marquis Hotels, 100
Marriott Residence Inn 17
Marriott at Sawgrass 52, 53, 54
Marriott's Bay Point Resort 34, 35
Marriott's Orlando World Center 18, 68, 69
Marsh Landing Country Club 51
McCumber, Mark 13, 22, 46, 55, 96, 100, 138
Meadowood 134
MetroWest 137
MetroWest Country Club 76
Miami Lakes Inn 108, 126, 142
Miami Springs Country Club 134
Mikita, Stan 34
Minelli, Liza 121
Mission Inn Golf & Tennis Resort 17, 58, 60, 61,
    142
Mission Inn Golf School 142
Mitchell, Bill 92
Mizner, Addison 114
Monroe County Tourist Development Council
    141
Mount Plymouth Golf Club 76
Murphy, Eddie 116
Muszak, Jim 24
N
Naples Area Chamber of Commerce 140
Naples Beach Hotel & Golf Club, 98
National Golf Foundation 13, 90, 91, 137, 141
Navarre, Carl 128
Nestle Invitational 57
Newman, Paul 128
Nichols, Bobby 91
Nicklaus, Jack 13, 57, 73, 108, 124, 128, 138, 139
Norman, Greg 57, 74
North Florida PGA Passport Card 18, 19, 141
O
Oak Ford 106
Ocala-Marion County Chamber of Commerce
    140
Oldsmobile LPGA Classic 141

Olney Inn 128
Orange Lake Country Club 18
Overton, Jay 88
Owen, Bill 139
P
PGA Merchandise Show 57
PGA National 137
PGA Seniors Championship 142
PGA Sheraton Resort 124
PGA Tour 40, 55, 57, 141
PGA Tour Qualifying School 34
Packard, E. Lawrence 87
Palm Beach County Convention and Visitors
    Bureau 141
Palm Beach Lakes Golf Club 134
Palm Beach Polo & Country Club 20, 112, 113,
    136
Palm Coast 41, 137
Palm-Aire Spa Resort 17
Palmer, Arnold 13, 41, 48, 57, 75, 80, 124, 138
Panama City Beach Classic 141
Panama City Visitors and Convention Bureau
    140
Pate, Jerry 36, 38, 53, 112, 113
Patrick Air Force Base Golf Course 76
Paulucci, Jeno 138
Peabody Orlando 17
Pebble Beach 40
Pebble Beach, Lodge at 50
Peete, Calvin 91
Pelican Bay 137, 138
Pelican Country Club 84
Pelican's Nest Golf Club 106
Pensacola Open 142
Pensacola Visitors & Convention Bureau 140
Perdido Bay Resort 22, 30
Perdido Beach Hilton 30
Phar-Mor Inverrary Classic 141
Pinellas Suncoast Tourist Development Council
    140
Plant, Henry B. 84
Plantation Golf & Country Club 102, 103
Plantation Inn & Golf Resort 82, 83, 142
Player, Gary 13, 57
Polane, Ron 114
Ponce De Leon Resort 55
Ponte Vedra Beach, The Lodge at 50, 51
Ponte Vedra Inn & Club 42
Price, Nick 57, 74
Professional Golfers Association 91, 108
Professional Golfers Association of America 141
R
Ravines Golf & Country Club 19, 46, 47
Real Estate Research Consultants Inc. 139
Redman, John 57
Refram, Dean 80
Regal Retreats 18, 141
Rinker, Larry 57
Ritson, Phil 57
River Wilderness 91
River's Edge Yacht & Country Club 106
Rogers, Kenny 122
Rolling Hills Golf Resort 133
Ross, Donald 55, 84, 91, 111
Royal Caribbean Classic 141
S
Saddlebrook 18, 19, 79, 80, 81, 136
Sam Snead Executive Golf Course 76
Sandestin Resort 32, 33, 136
Sanibel-Captiva Island Chamber of Commerce
    141
Sarasota County Chamber of Commerce 141
Sauers, Becky 28
Sawgrass 20, 53, 136, 137
Schultze, Leonard 110

Seascape Resort 38
Seay, Ed 13, 48, 51, 53, 62, 138
Sebring Golf School 142
Seminole 19
Seminole Golf Club 38
Senior Golfer 142
Shalimar Pointe Golf & Country Club 38
Sheraton Bonaventure Resort & Spa 20, 116, 142
Sheraton Palm Coast Resort 18, 48
Shoal River Golf & Country Club 38
Shula, Don 126
Sinatra, Frank 114, 122
Snead, Sam 114
Sonesta Sanibel Harbor Resort 17
South Seas Plantation 94, 95
Spalding Space Coast Tour 57
St. Augustine & St. Johns County Chamber of
    Commerce 140
St. Augustine Shores Golf Course 55
St. Leo Abbey Golf Club 89
St. Lucie West 137
Stewart, Payne 57, 74
Stockton, Jim 42
Strange, Curtis 30
Summer Beach Resort & Country Club 55
Summerfield Golf Club 89
Sun City Center 142
Sundial Beach Resort, 100, 101
T
Tallahassee Convention & Visitors Bureau 140
Tampa Palms Golf & Country Club 137
Tampa/Hillsborough Convention and Visitors
    Association 18, 140
Tatum Ridge 106
Taylor, Elizabeth 121
Team Championship 142
Tee Times Magazine 142
The Club at Hidden Creek 38
The Meadows 106
The Nestle Invitational 142
The Players Championship 141
Tiger Point Golf & Country Club 38
Timacuan Golf & Country Club 76
Tournament Players Club at Sawgrass Stadium
    Course 13, 20, 22, 52, 53, 54
Trevino, Lee 23, 75
Turnberry Isle 108, 118, 119
Twitchell, Carl 128
Twitchell, Cynthia 128
U
U.S. Open 25
United States Golf Card Association 141
V
Ventura Country Club 76
Venturi, Ken 91
Villas of Grand Cypress 74
Vince Cali Golf Schools 142
Von Hagge, Robert 34, 106, 120, 131
W
Walt Disney World Classic 57, 142
Wallace, Mike 91
Walt Disney World Conference Center 65
Walt Disney World Golf Studio 57, 65, 142
Walt Disney World Resort 17, 19, 57, 64, 142
Watkins family, 98
Watts, Bill 126
Wee Links, 64
Weston 138
Wild Dunes 20
Wildcat Run 106
Williams, Ted 139
Wilson, Dick 22, 75, 106, 130,
Windstar 91
Winter Pines Golf Club 76
World of Golf 17, 141